meant
to be

meant to be

LISA FAULKNER

EBURY
PRESS

This edition published in 2020 by Ebury Press,
an imprint of Ebury Publishing
20 Vauxhall Bridge Road
London SW1V 2SA

1 3 5 7 9 10 8 6 4 2

Ebury Press is part of the Penguin Random House
group of companies whose addresses can be found
at global.penguinrandomhouse.com

Penguin
Random House
UK

First published by Ebury Press in 2019

www.penguin.co.uk

A CIP catalogue record for this book is available from the British Library

ISBN 9781529104158

Printed and bound in Great Britain by Clays Ltd, Elcograf S.p.A.

Penguin Random House is committed to a sustainable future
for our business, our readers and our planet. This book is
made from Forest Stewardship Council® certified paper.

MIX
Paper from
responsible sources
FSC® C018179

To my daughter Billie.

And to you, the reader, I hope I provide a hand to hold and a sigh of relief that there is no right or wrong on the sometimes bumpy path to motherhood. Whatever route you take will lead you to where you're meant to be.

There is a hole in the sky
Where the light falls through
Where the whole of me
Is the whole of you

Lemn Sissay MBE

Prologue

My sister and I pulled up into the large grey car park of the Mothercare superstore. She was six months pregnant and her perfect bump was now properly showing; she looked radiant.

It was raining and cold, but not even the weather could dampen my excitement. Today we were going shopping for baby things, but instead of it being for her child, this time it was for me. It was for my baby and I could hardly believe it was finally happening. My time had finally arrived and I was going to Embrace it with a capital E!

This was the first time in a long while that I'd allowed myself to feel happy, to actually feel the joy. Yes, I felt trepidation at what was to come; after all, I was shopping for a toddler I had never met. I knew I would always feel a slight pang that I wasn't there as a pregnant person, that I hadn't managed to grow a baby, but essentially I had made my peace with it. I had done as much mental preparation as I could possibly do and I was truly excited to take this next step into motherhood, my own unique way of mothering. So for now, I gave myself over to this moment. I took a deep breath and smiled. I deserved to enjoy this.

My sister Victoria was beside herself too, so happy to finally be able to share in my joy. For what had seemed like an eternity, she'd listened to me as I cried at my failure to become a mother. She'd sat up late into the night with me and talked on the phone for hours, feeling frustrated that she couldn't do anything to make it better. It had been so hard to watch her fall pregnant for the third time at the drop of a hat, and I remember storming out of her house when she told me her happy news, screaming at her about the unfairness of it all. It had taken a long time and a lot of soul searching to adjust my frame of mind and be OK with doing things a different way and, through all of this, my sister had stood firmly beside me, holding my hand.

All her own baby stuff had been bought and confidently put away in drawers after two textbook conceptions and pregnancies, but, finally, here she was for me, and pregnant for a third time herself. I had a list as long as my arm of things I needed and, although I had a budget, now I was here, I had a feeling that was going straight out the window.

We walked through the doors into the heady bright lights and the warmth of the shop and, as my sister grabbed a trolley, I took in the scene around me. The place was full of women. There were a few men shuffling around, looking uncomfortable, but mainly all I could see were women in different phases of pregnancy, along with dozens of toddlers tearing around and babies wrapped snuggly in their buggies. It was a shop full of hope and life – nothing special to most of the people in it, but to me it was heaven on earth.

I had spent years leafing through baby catalogues for children's clothes, buying outfits in Baby Gap for the newborn babies of close friends, desperate for it to be my turn, always with my heart in my mouth and a tear threatening to escape. I felt I was doomed to be always the godmother.

It had taken me so long to get here, years of hoping and praying. Years of having sex at the right time, and then being heartbroken when my period arrived. Years of weeing on sticks, of having injections, of feeling like a failure when the blue line didn't magically appear. It had been a long, hard road of self-discovery and yet, even though I was at the end, it still wasn't exactly as I had planned. OK, I would never be full bellied and blooming, but I knew I would eventually be all right.

As I stood in that shop with my list, I was aware I had a long journey ahead of me, a different journey from all my friends and family, but a journey nonetheless, and it was mine. I was headed straight for the toddler aisles, shopping for a little girl I had not yet met, and one that I didn't know if I would get to keep. I took a deep breath, and smiled. I was apprehensive and scared, but as I kept telling myself, this was my day and I was determined to make the most of it.

It's very strange shopping for a child you don't know – though in many ways I suppose it's exactly the same as shopping for a newborn. You have no idea of its personality and all you can do is pick the stuff that catches your eye. Here is a good time to say that I had never thought of myself as a girlie girl. In my daydreams, my baby's nursery was white and clean with lots of different colours, but as I went to buy bedding and buggies, everything that caught my eye was pink! A pink changing mat, a pink and grey buggy, pink duvet set, pink cot bumpers, pink pink pink! I caught my sister staring at me, open mouthed, out of the corner of my eye.

'What?' I said.

'Nothing. Just didn't ever see you as that sort of mum, all pink and fluffy! But enjoy!'

I grinned back.

As I picked out sleep suits and dummies and plates and spouty cups, chatting away to my sister about what bottles would be best and discussing whether my little girl would need shoes, my insecurities began to surface.

'What if we don't get to keep her?' I said anxiously.

'We've been through this. If you don't keep her, you will have given her stability, love, warmth and security when she needed it most. She can take all these things with her and you will have helped her so much.'

'Yes,' I sighed. 'You're right. Thank God for you.'

Victoria had been my rock throughout this long adoption path, even agreeing to go on all the adoption courses for friends and family. It had been a real eye-opener for her. We had all been told what to expect, what to do and say and, more importantly, what not to say. The main thing was never to give false hope to either the parents who were adopting, or the child coming into the family. It was drummed into us that we had to deal in absolutes, and yet there was nothing certain about any part of the process and I had already suffered so much disappointment. I was only just getting my head around all of this and it meant so much that she was next to me, supporting me through everything. My wonderful sister, with her words of encouragement, so desperate for me to be happy and to have my chance to be a mum.

My husband had been happy to let the two of us go it alone for our girlie/mummy shopping day, knowing how very much this everyday rite of passage meant to me. And, as we started shopping for all these 'magical' things, I couldn't help but think how much my mum would have loved this day – she would have been with us, chatting and shopping and offering her advice. How wonderful it would have been to share it all with her.

I think my dad had found it really hard to see me suffering so badly. As a father, you always want to fix things for your little girl and this – like my mum's death – was something he definitely had no control over. Seeing us grieve for our mum was bad enough, but seeing me grieve for a baby I never had was also heartbreaking. Now, for the first time in a while, he too had allowed himself a chink of happiness, and he was delighted that he was potentially going to be a grandad yet again!

It felt so weird to experience all these feelings for a girl I hadn't met yet, a girl who was going to change my life forever. I had seen just one photo; I had never heard her voice or smelled her hair. I thought back to the conversation we'd had with the social worker, to the first time we had seen a picture of her – her little pixie face with huge eyes and a cheeky smile.

My heart had melted. My girl had been described as a ray of sunshine, full of energy. And now she would be moving in, in a matter of weeks. I prayed that she would like all of this. I prayed that I could be the mother that she so desperately needed. I prayed that she would like me …

It was all very real to me now. Parenthood had finally come to me, in a roundabout way of course, but here it was. Adoption wasn't the route I dreamed that I would go down, and it isn't the way we are traditionally taught that families are made, but none of that mattered to me now. My life had already shown me I wasn't necessarily going to take a 'normal' path and here I was, creating my own family, but just in a different way. This was going to be my different kind of perfect.

Chapter 1

When people find out the lengths I went to in order to become a mother they always assume I have been obsessed with babies my whole life. But that couldn't be further from the truth. Actually, I didn't ever really want a baby when I was younger, and I certainly wasn't one of those girls who dreamed of pushing a pram. Deep down, I suppose I assumed it would happen one day, but that was a long way off and I had a lot of life to live first.

Despite this, when I was really young, my sister and I would play with our Tiny Tears dolls. Dressing them up, putting them in prams and wheeling them around chatting. We mindlessly re-enacted what our mother (and her friends who had babies) had done, but I don't think we gave it much thought. It was just one of the many games we played, along with Barbies and gypsies and ballet dancers. It was a rite of passage, I suppose, a game lots of girls play, an unspoken language and a club we all assumed we would one day become a part of. It was a given. And so from the age of eight until about 28, I didn't really give it much thought.

The story my mum always told when people asked her about us was that she never really wanted children at first. She used to say quite loudly that it was my dad who wanted us, and she wasn't worried either way. This is something that makes me smile now, seeing as it became such a mission for me to have children, and my own mother said she would have been just fine with a life without children. I also smile because I know that when she had us everything changed; she would do anything for us and we really became her life, and I wonder how and why she had such bravado.

My dad and my godmothers have all said that my mum was adamant that, if she were to have children, then she wanted girls. Family legend has it that she tried several old wives' superstitions to make sure she only had female babies. She was a true royalist, so it didn't surprise me to hear from my godmother that she followed the royal family's secret of how to conceive girls. (I have no idea what this was, by the way, or how she came to find out about it, or if it was in any way true – but it obviously worked!)

When Victoria and I came along, as I said, everything changed. It's strange and sometimes really gets to me that I can't ask my mother what she truly thought about having us and how she mothered us when we were babies. I have to get it second-hand from my dad, my auntie and my godmothers. But I also know that a large part of her mothering is automatically instilled in me, and so much of what comes naturally is learned behaviour, spilling out into Billie's life now.

When I look back at baby photos, it's clear how very much my mother loved me. It just shines out of her. There are dozens of photos of her smiling at me, and very distant, sketchy memories of her biting my toes and making me laugh. Nothing was too much trouble. When my mum put her mind to anything, she did it 100 per cent and we were no exception! I know that she bottle-fed me (it was the seventies and a new fad), and from conversations with my auntie, she took everything in her stride. She took to motherhood like a duck to water, and anything she didn't know she made up as she went along.

My auntie Susan (my dad's sister) and my mum were really close and she tells a great story from when I was about three months old and my auntie was nine months pregnant with my cousin. I was still in a carrycot and my mum had put me in the boot of her Renault 4 – a perfectly acceptable place for a baby at the time. My auntie was in the passenger seat and a car went into the back of them. My mum got out of the car shouting, 'I have a baby in the boot and my friend here is just about to drop!' Apparently the man, who had (very lightly) bumped into her, didn't know what had hit him and, after giving him what for, my mum and auntie laughed and laughed at how terrified he had been. This describes my mother to a tee. Fiercely protective and loyal, she was a lioness whose bark was worse than her bite, and whose anger dissipated very quickly, leaving laughter in its place.

My mum was always out with me; having a new baby never got in her way. She and my auntie were constantly going on day trips or having lunch. Auntie Susan also tells me that my cousin often wished that my mum had been his mum, as coming round to ours was always exciting. My mum never cared about mess (she was the untidiest person I know) and we were always painting at the kitchen table, or gluing feathers on pictures or baking and making pastry. Apparently she would make my party decorations and spend hours making incredible themed birthday cakes. In fact she would do anything rather than keep the house tidy! I wish I had more memories of these times. It's lovely to hear these stories and I know that my mother gave me the most stable foundations and shaped me into the person I am today. I was always safe, always warm and always loved. These were gifts I was desperate to hand on to my own child in any way I could.

I am lucky to have a sister. Victoria was born when I was nearly two years old and we have always been inseparable. There are actually only 22 months between my sister and me; I think my mother probably planned it that way so that we would have each other to play with and turn to, something she missed out on greatly herself, being an only child. I also think she knew it meant that we would entertain each other and free up some of her own time!

Nearly every memory I have of growing up is of me and my sister, my mum and dad and our dog. Our childhood really was pretty idyllic and whenever I feel small or worried about things I think back fondly to our house and our times together as a family. We were very secure. We grew up in Esher in Surrey; my dad was a civil servant and my mother a legal secretary and, when we came along, our mum worked part time to spend more hours with us. We lived in a nice house on a nice street. We weren't rich and we weren't poor, very much the middle of the road. There were a lot of times growing up when we didn't have very much money but we always got by.

My mum was a brilliant cook and the house was always warm and smelled of something appetising! We would do our homework at the kitchen table while my mum made dinner and waited for my dad to come back from work.

My sister and I were never lonely and, although we had best friends of our own, we often played together as children. We had an old brick 'larder' just outside the kitchen, which at one point probably housed the loo. It now contained shelves crammed with pots of all different paints and glues, ice-cream tubs full of bits and pieces we could stick onto our home-made artwork and old rolls of wallpaper that were perfect for making posters. This cupboard was often used in our games of make-believe. We would stand outside it with our babies in buggies, gossiping like grown-ups and pretending it was a lift in a shop. In and out we would go all morning! Or it was a shop in itself and we would chat about our babies and feed them while looking at the shelves. Always with our babies, always together.

I remember school holidays and weekends just flying by as we made dens or houses and played with Sindy dolls, endlessly dressing them up and cutting their hair short to make some of them into boyfriends. We would go upstairs to our bedrooms and literally create a whole world. We had an old wooden chest that was our dressing-up box, full of our mum's cast-aside clothes and things we had found at jumble sales. We would be singers or dancers or fortune-telling gypsies in old caravans, which in reality were our bunk beds draped with sheets and blankets.

Downstairs, we had a large front room that was saved for best. At one point in its life it housed our dining-room table, a shiny, mahogany, well-polished oval. I remember us watching Torvill and Dean ice-skate to Ravel's *Boléro* for the 1984 Olympics. My mother was obsessed by them. One day my sister and I decided to re-enact it and what better place than the table to be our ice rink? We had woollen tights on which were perfect for skating. We were having a brilliant time until my sister managed to skate along the top of the table and smashed into an antique vase on the windowsill. We got into so much trouble because of the vase (not because we could have really hurt ourselves!) and, looking back now, I wonder how my mother kept a straight face while giving us a proper telling off.

Other times, my sister and I would put on the soundtrack to *Grease* or *Cats* or *Evita* and sing our way through each song, giving each other marks out of ten and getting dressed up ready for our next performance. I wonder if my parents ever spied on us singing our little hearts out. I know I would if it was Billie now! My mum wouldn't see us until we ventured down for dinner, starving or squabbling because the other one had got bored with the game. Obviously at times we argued;

life wasn't all rosy. We were either up or down – there was no in between, and if we weren't playing nicely and giggling like loons then we were fighting, biting, scratching and wishing each other dead. My mother took it in her stride, knowing that it would all blow over and we would be friends again in a matter of minutes.

We were very close to my grandparents who doted on us, and on Sundays my granddad would cycle over and bring us great slabs of chocolate and all sorts of goodies. He would tell us ghost stories about Hampton Court Palace where he worked as a glazier, or funny anecdotes about the people he met at the British Legion, or we would beg him to tell us a story about when he was little, or about the war. He would regale us with tales, some of which my mum would dispute or say never happened. My mum would cook lunch and my grandparents would come over for a big family meal. In fact, my nanna was over at ours a lot as I was growing up; she would get the bus and come in and literally clean the house top to bottom. As I said, my mum was super messy and Nanna would make everything look lovely, only for us to mess it all up again!

If my mum wasn't cooking lunch, we would go out for the day, taking a picnic with us. Dull and rainy weekends were my mum's worst enemy (and became mine too in later life) so at the first sign of sunshine we would be packed off into the car to visit a stately home or National Trust park. My sister and I would dread these visits to places like Polesden Lacey and Goodwood House. We would be rolling our eyes at our parents from the back of the car, moaning about how boring it was going to be. We would wander round the house and the grounds, reluctantly at first, but then, after the initial sullen faces, our imaginations would take over and we would create some game where we were either the maids or the lady of the house and these were our rooms. Or we would pretend to be foreign tourists and talk in our made-up language at each other, thinking we were fooling everyone. We would spend the whole day exploring the old houses and grounds and stop off for a cup of tea and a piece of cake in the tearoom before we left. What's funny is that, for all the moaning about going, I actually now realise we loved it, and those memories totally shape who I am today and what I do with my daughter. Whenever I bundle her into the car to go somewhere similar and she tells me how boring it's going to be, I smile because I know that she enjoys it when she is there, and I know these memories will live with her forever.

My mum really loved to entertain. Any excuse to make dinner or lunch and have people round and she would immediately be planning menus and deciding what to cook and what theme a dinner party would take. She had a very close group of friends, much like I do now, and they would take it in turns to host dinner parties that always ended up with them dancing and drinking and laughing so loudly that all the children who were staying over at ours would be awake upstairs. We would listen in to their raucous stories and whisper excitedly about whose parent had drunk the most or danced the most crazily. I remember one time we peeked through the keyhole of the front room to see my parents and their friends doing a dance to 'Oops Up Side Your Head' on the floor, in absolute hysterics. We would often take advantage of their distraction to sneak into the dining room with its abandoned pavlova or profiteroles and quickly eat as much as we could before racing back up the stairs at the sound of a parent coming to check on us, and pretending to be asleep. My mum's pavlova was a showstopper, a dessert that features in so many of my childhood memories. Whether sneaked upstairs or eaten the next morning from the spot it had stayed in overnight, it was never less than delicious. It's crispy on the outside and chewy in the middle and will always remind me of my childhood. I'll give you the recipe at the end of this chapter.

My mum always said that she treated my sister and me in exactly the same way. She dressed us in the same outfits until I was about eight, when I put up too much of a fight and she eventually gave in and let me wear my own clothes. She wanted us to feel that we were equal in everything. She never bought anything for one of us without buying something equivalent for the other and I even seem to remember my sister getting a present on my birthdays so that she wasn't left out!

I remember my mum saying that my sister, who went to drama classes, could be an actress and I could be a French teacher because I was good at French. I felt very stung by this at the time: my sister the flamboyant, exciting actress and me the boring French teacher. My mother said it purely to show us our strengths and, I think, in the hope that we wouldn't want to pursue the same dream and compete with each other

– but at the time I just felt hurt. As I got older I thought that my mum definitely favoured my sister. However, looking back on it now, I think it was my hormones and general moodiness that made this seem the case. Whenever I was grumpy, my sister would become the model child and play right into my mum's hands while I sulked even further, scowling through my fringe at the pair of them.

Hindsight is a wonderful thing, and so is being a mother myself. As I enter the teenage years with Billie, I see so much of myself in her. I also see that my behaviour was nothing out of the ordinary and no different from that of any other teenage girl with hormones flying everywhere. I can now see that the ups and downs my mum and I had were all completely normal and my perception that she loved my sister more was very much unfounded. She was just trying to do her best. In any case, I think at different times you do favour different children; it's just a fact of life that some days one may seem better behaved and more easy-going than the other.

I was very lucky in that, as well as having my mother, I also grew up with a small army of strong women all around me, loving, mothering and shaping me. For example, there was my great-auntie Elsie, my nanna's sister. She was a good few years older than my nanna and, although she had given birth to a stillborn baby in her twenties, she had never gone on to have any more children of her own. Auntie Elsie doted on us. She adored my mum too and we frequently had her to stay. Mummy always said that Elsie was like a second mother to her, very similar to the relationship that I have with my nieces and nephew now. I think about Elsie often these days, and how when I was a child I had no idea of the loss and grief she had suffered. To me she was a kind old lady who said funny things and I couldn't in any way identify with the pain she must have experienced in her youth. Years later here I am thinking about her, and understanding fully the extent of her grief, of her loss and sadness at not having children. As I type, I whisper up a little prayer of love to her. Had she been alive while I was going through my journey to motherhood, I think she would have been the one who would have understood the most.

My nanna was my mum's mum. Soon after Nanna gave birth to her, doctors discovered huge fibroids in her womb and after having them removed she couldn't have any more children. So my mum became her pride and joy; she was thoroughly spoiled and when we came along it followed that we were too! Nanna would let us make dens and play schools and all sorts of games, never making us tidy anything up after ourselves. She would just let us do whatever we wanted. We baked with her, made Coke floats and ate hundreds of drop scones and pancakes with whatever toppings we wanted. She taught us how to spring clean, how to look after things, how to sew and how to be kind. She was a really strong, beautiful woman and we loved to listen to her stories of her growing up, as everything seemed so cosy in the olden days. I now wish I had shared the ups and downs of my IVF with her, but I wanted to protect her from it all. I think we don't give older people enough credit sometimes – we concentrate on wanting to shelter them, treating them as if they are babies. I know

now that she would have been a really good person to go to for advice.

Then there was Betty, my dad's mum. She always thought she was too young to be a grandmother, hence she was called by her first name! She was younger than Nanna and fun in a very different way. She and my grandfather lived in West Sussex very near the sea. Betty taught us to cook as well and to knit but she also taught us the naughty things. She would tell us all the gossip of the street and give us great detail about the books she was reading, tales of illicit affairs and murders and ghosts. She loved a Cinzano at 'elevenses' and another at five o'clock while watching *Blockbusters*. She did crosswords and puzzles and we were always doing something. Even on rainy days we were bustled outside in rain macs and jumpers and told to go and play, and we would entertain ourselves for hours at the old abandoned farm across the road or make dens in their large back garden.

These amazing women all shaped me into the person I am today, warts and all. The main thing they taught me was love. How to love and be loved. How to talk about things and stand up for myself. None of them were wallflowers. They all had something to say and a great voice to say it with. I wish that my daughter had met them, as they would have adored her. She was lucky enough to have my nanna in her life for her first six years and she has very fond memories and a bank of stories she still tells about her.

I am also lucky enough to have my auntie and my 'godmothers', my mum's three best friends. They too have always been there for me, together creating a support network that I have undoubtedly mirrored with my own tribe of friends, a unit that keeps the cycle going for my own daughter.

As I write I see a pattern of women, of family and nurture, of make-believe and extraordinary support. I feel very blessed having these people and these wonderful memories. At the time I had no idea of the importance of such a loving childhood, or that life could turn on a sixpence and change so drastically.

My mum's pavlova
Serves 6

You will need:
3 egg whites
A pinch of salt
250g caster sugar
1 tsp vanilla extract
1 tsp malt vinegar
300ml double cream
1 x 400g tin of raspberries in syrup or juice
250g fresh strawberries, hulled and sliced
250g fresh raspberries

Method:
Preheat the oven to 140°C/gas mark 1. Draw and cut out a 23cm circle on baking parchment (use a cake tin as a guide) and place on a baking tray.

Using a handheld electric mixer, whisk the egg whites and salt until stiff, then gradually add the sugar. Keep whisking until the mixture reaches the glossy stiff peak stage, then fold in the vanilla extract and vinegar.

Spread the meringue mixture over the circle of baking parchment and bake in the oven for 1 hour until firm. My mum's trick, which I believe is the key to the perfect meringue, was to turn off the oven and leave the meringue in there with the door closed for another half an hour after it has cooked.

Leave to cool, peel off the baking parchment and place on a serving plate.

Whip the cream until stiff, then pile on top of the meringue. Strain the tinned raspberries and place in the centre of the pavlova then arrange the fresh fruit on top.

Eat immediately but it is also really good as gooey leftovers the next day.

Chapter 2

My diary, Monday 12 December 1988

Mummy died this morning.
I can't believe it.
She's still my lovely mummy.
I'll always love her.

Sometimes I think it's mad that someone I knew for only 16 years of my life defines me so completely and utterly. Within me lies my mother, her essence and all the things she taught me and everything she was. She is the reason I sit here today, the reason I look the way I do and act the way I do, genetically and existentially, if that makes sense.

And what a woman, what a force of nature Julie was. She was beautiful and wild and angry and kind. She was the most fun at parties and you could tell what mood she was in by the way she shut the front door. If Mummy was in a good mood the whole house was happy and there was no room for anyone bringing her down, but if she was in a bad mood, God help you! The doors would slam and Victoria and I would tiptoe around her, not wanting to say the wrong thing, just waiting for my dad to come home from work so they could talk and things would calm down.

I didn't ever expect Mummy to die. I couldn't comprehend it. Things like that happened to other people, not to me. Our life had seemed so normal up to that point: we grew up in a lovely house on a lovely street in suburbia and generally speaking my mum and dad were pretty happy. That said, they had massive rows sometimes – well, my mum had massive rows with my dad, who just quietly took it all on the chin. She would scream and shout and stomp around and he would just listen and placate her until the storm was over and Mummy was calm and back to normal.

I make it sound like she was really angry and stroppy. She wasn't like that all the time. And when she was happy the sun came out and shone on everyone around her. I think, like me, she worried all the time about everything, and sometimes things got her down. Ironically, my mum's biggest fear was getting cancer.

This was the eighties and there was definitely more of a stigma about cancer than there is now. In fact, she wouldn't even use the word in our house. My mummy really was a force of nature, a whirlwind and she was always very, very much *alive*, if that makes sense. Her getting cancer and dying seemed completely impossible, not only to me, but to everyone who knew her. We all felt the world would stop turning without her in it.

I was 15 when my mum first became ill. I had only recently hit puberty and was suddenly discovering boys and wanting to go out, and I hate to say it, but her illness was pretty inconvenient for me at the time.

It started with an ulcer on her tongue that wouldn't go away. She kept going back to the dentist, and he kept sending her home, saying that it was nothing. I think it took quite a while before he actually listened to her and sent her to the doctor. She had tests and the doctors said it was cancer, but they thought that they could cut it out and zap it with radiotherapy. She had to go into hospital for a whole week and, because of the radiation, no one was allowed to go into her room. There was a window at the door and all my sister and I could do was wave at her through it. It was horrible seeing her in a hospital bed, putting on a brave face and waving back at us. I know I was really frightened for her and worried, but in my diary, I referred to it as a 'cancer thing' so I don't think I really understood what was happening, especially as my mum and dad outwardly seemed very positive about it all.

Life continued pretty normally after that. Mummy got better and I continued to go out to the pub with my friends!! And my whole world went back to revolving around me. Mummy seemed fine and our relationship became tricky: I was a teenager who wanted to be out all the time and we clashed. At the time I was so angry with her and she was angry with me (all the usual mother–daughter stuff that happens at that age, and that I am now going through with my own daughter). I also think that, although we thought she was better, actually she was still unwell and trying to cope with that, and having a stroppy teenager didn't help things.

About six months later, my mum started feeling properly ill again. Her neck was hurting, and Daddy bought her one of those heat lamps that she would sit with. She was in real pain and went back to the doctor, where they did tests and found that there was a lump in her neck.

They said this was a result of not catching the ulcer in time, but that it was fixable. So, she had an operation to remove the lump and a five-week course of radiotherapy. The following six months seemed really good and, although Mummy and I argued, we also had fun – life was full of feasts at Henley regatta and people coming over for parties. We had a lovely holiday in Portugal and, although Mummy was OK, I remember thinking that she didn't seem herself. She was preoccupied and a bit far away.

Sure enough, when we returned home she went to see the specialist and, again, they found the cancer had spread, this time to her throat. I knew this was getting serious but, at that age, I had no idea what to do with my feelings. So instead of crying and spending time with my family, I went to the pub with my friends and wrote pages and pages in my diary obsessing about boyfriends – diverting all my attention onto them and studying (sporadically) for my GCSEs.

Rightly or wrongly, my parents decided not to tell us too much and we were really protected from what was actually going on. I remember them playing it down and, as a result, we weren't ever really sure how serious it was.

My mum had a course of chemotherapy that went well, and she was back to her old self for a bit. However, it was pretty short lived. In October 1988, she went back into hospital for a second round of chemotherapy but she had an allergic reaction to the drugs and ended up in a coma for a few days.

It all felt so surreal, as if it wasn't really happening to us. When she came round she had such difficulty breathing that they decided to do a tracheotomy. At this time, although I didn't know it until a while later, Mummy knew she was very ill and I think she had almost given up, especially as she was in so much pain. In hospital she wrote letters to me and Victoria, just in case she died. My dad gave them to us much later on and I keep her letter with me all the time. If there was one item that I would save in a fire it would be that letter; it's the one thing I have in her handwriting that was written especially for me.

In that letter I realised how much she loved me (something I didn't always think at the time). She gave me advice and told me that she was so very proud of me. The little girl inside me still reads that letter and gains strength from it in my dark hours.

At this time, I was still going out a lot and trying to revise for a resit of my failed maths GCSE, but an element of guilt had crept in, that somehow this was my fault. Maybe I was such a bad daughter and so self-obsessed that I had brought on this cancer. I write in my diary about going to see teachers and crying and asking them if that could be possible, if it could be my fault. I carried this guilt around for years.

I remember pretty much every detail of the days before Mummy died – it's so weird what memory does. I remember that the Friday before I pretended I was sick so I could stay home from school. My godmother Nina arrived to sit with my mum (who by this time was always in bed). I lay in my bed and listened in on their conversation. Nina read my mum some poems and together they sorted through her jewellery, separating the good pieces from the costume stuff into different wash bags for later. I could hear them discussing what was to go to who. I knew then that things were really serious and yet still I couldn't quite admit it to myself. If only I could have that time again, if only I could have sat with her and read her poetry and talked to her. There are so many things about her that I will never know because I never got to ask.

On the Sunday night I went to the cinema to see *Who Framed Roger Rabbit?* I didn't want to leave her but I went. That night I came home and prayed to God that she would be OK. The next morning, I woke up and decided I wasn't going to school; instead I would meet my boyfriend and study at the library. I went in to say goodbye to Mummy. She was quite drugged up with all the morphine, but I remember that, as I gave her a kiss, she squeezed my hand. I didn't know that that was the last time I would see her alive.

Apparently, a few minutes after we left for school, Daddy went into her room. She was meant to be going to the hospital that day for another round of chemo. He was getting a few things ready for her on the bed when he realised that she had stopped breathing. He always said he knew she would have been happy to die in her own bed. Not in an ambulance or in hospital, having chemo, with her hair falling out. She was very proud and she would have hated that to be her final moment.

What happened next was a bit of a blur. My boyfriend and I drove round looking for a library to study in but they were all shut on a Monday in our area. We decided to head back home and, as we got to the top of my road, everything seemed to slow down. I saw my uncle in his car, I waved at him and he gave me the oddest look. We stopped the car outside my house and I remember walking up that garden path so slowly, almost knowing that I was going to open the door to something I didn't want to. As I put my key in the door my granddad was standing there. He said to me: 'Daddy's been looking for you. He's gone to school to find you. Mummy's upstairs.'

'What? Is she OK?' I said, and he replied so starkly: 'No. She's dead.'

I pushed past him and ran up the stairs (I have no memory of what happened to my boyfriend, whether he stayed or left, or whether anyone else was there). She was lying in her bed, just as I had left her a few hours earlier. She looked so peaceful and I just got into bed with her, under the covers, and held her. My beautiful mummy. Still warm, still there but not there, her pain finally gone. I don't know how long I stayed like that, just holding her and crying from a place so deep inside me that I didn't know existed.

I am not sure that grief will ever really go away. I am not sure that I want it to, as letting go of that is letting go of my mummy and I will never do that.

As I reread what I have written in my teenage diary, I am struck by my 16-year-old self's thoughts and guilt. I would like to hold her tight and tell her that none of it is her fault, that it is just life and that she will get up again. She will be OK. This leads me straight to my thoughts on motherhood. Immediately I want to mother the teenager in me. That force is so strong.

I wonder what my mum would have made of my life now. How she would have coped with my infertility, with me adopting. I know that she would have loved Billie; she would have recognised that free spirit that is so much a part of her and she would have spoiled her rotten. I am so very sad that she never got the chance to meet my girl. Instead I regale Billie with stories about Grandma Julie and I think she knows so much about her that she would be sure to recognise her in another dimension. I have done my best to bring her alive for Billie, but of course it isn't the same as having her here, being part of everything and influencing Billie in the way that she did me.

I wonder, if my mum hadn't died, whether my need to be a mother would have been as great. I wonder if I have been trying to fill the huge gap left by her, to recreate something I was retrospectively lacking. I know at the time I didn't see this at all, but then I was buried by grief and not able to analyse anything in any detail. I think somewhere inside me, I felt that, if I could be a mother and recreate the things mine did with me, then I would definitely feel close to her again. I think that maybe I am always subconsciously looking for ways to reconnect with her even though she isn't here any more. I have definitely done that with my cooking career, especially when it comes to the fact that I have all her utensils and cooking equipment in my kitchen today. In my head, if I could be a mother, then I would be closer to her in some way. My childhood felt so perfect and stable and I think I have grieved for that, as well as my mum, at times. The need to have that back in my life in some way must definitely be linked to me wanting to nurture and be a mother myself.

I would love to have two conversations with my mother. Well, I would like a million but, if I could only have two, the first would be about my infertility. I would love to have asked her advice. I am not sure I would have wanted children any less if I'd been able to talk to her about it, but then again maybe I would. Seeing as she apparently hadn't been bothered about whether she had children or not, would she have led me down a different path? Would she have told me that I didn't need children in order to be happy? Would she have told me about the other life she could have lived had we not come along? Or would she have grabbed my wrists and looked deep into my soul and said: 'You do it, Lisa, whatever it takes. You try everything you can to get your child because you will make a wonderful mother and you have so very much to give and I have loved every moment of being your mother.'

The second conversation would be to tell her that I understand. That now, being the mother of a teenager, I get it.

LISA FAULKNER

I see why we were always at loggerheads; I see how I pushed her buttons. I would tell her I love her and I know that she loved me and that, had we been lucky enough to get through those teenage years, we would be out the other side in the sun, linking arms, her telling me with a smile: 'Be careful what you wish for,' and offering me words of encouragement and advice that this too shall pass.

So what effect has this had on me as a mother? It definitely made me yearn to be one. Maybe to recreate for someone else the safe and happy childhood that stood me in such good stead. Maybe to right the wrongs. My mum wasn't a cuddly, mumsy mummy and I definitely am and always wanted to be. I always smell of baking whereas she always smelled of Christian Dior, even though she spent hours in the kitchen! I know that we definitely didn't have the communication that I have with my daughter and I was scared to talk to my mum about certain things. Maybe it's a sign of changing times, but I would never have talked to my mother about sex or boys. I was always scared to tell her if something had happened at school in case she thought I was somehow to blame.

When I was in Year Six I got terribly bullied by two girls who were supposed to be my best friends. Every day they would push me in the mud on our school field. They would push me from one to the other, my white socks filthy and wet with mud. Every day I would come home with a different excuse as to why this had happened. Terrified to tell my mum the real truth, as I knew she would be up at that school in a flash, but also because I was scared that she wouldn't believe me. In the end my sister threatened to beat the two of them up and they soon stopped!

Billie and I talk about everything, no holds barred. I have made sure that she isn't scared to talk to me, that she can say pretty much anything and I won't be fazed. Believe me, I am not naïve enough to think that there won't be a time when she withholds information from me, but I hope she will always know that I will rarely shout and never judge, and there is nothing that she could tell me that would shock me. I think I have consciously made the decision to be the mother I am, to learn from my relationship with my mother and to do some things differently from her. I also think that, mostly, I parent in the same way as I would have done had I given birth to my daughter. There is obviously that extra factor that adoption brings but fundamentally I am the mother that I thought I would be.

As an adoptive mum, your default position is always to question yourself and your parenting. Think about the scenario: a child you don't know moves into your home less than five days after your initial meeting (more on that later), and you are left alone with a tiny stranger. You have a few bits of knowledge about their likes and dislikes and an understanding of their (sometimes non-existent) routine and you are left to get on with it. So, right from the start, you are always questioning whether you are doing the right thing and parenting the right way. Yes, there are parenting classes and courses, but much like a first-time mother, you are really feeling your way and acting on your instincts. But with adoption there is always a plus. I definitely parent the way I would my own birth child most of the time, but I also have to be mindful of the life that Billie had before me, of the trauma and abandonment that an adopted child can sometimes have suffered.

So there are different ways of doing things and ways that raise the eyebrows of well-meaning friends and relatives, as maybe the 'naughty step' will not be an option for your child. I also think I am constantly mindful of her past and maybe, just maybe, I am more lenient with her than I would have been with my birth child. I still discipline and have proper boundaries, but sometimes I have to go about implementing them in a different way. It is a constant learning curve. With an adoptive child there are sometimes traits in them that you don't recognise and a face staring back at you that you can't immediately figure out. That can be hard, but also very liberating. You definitely have to put in a lot more work, but eventually you get the effort back tenfold.

My final thought is that my mother's death was my first introduction into life not being 'normal'. It was not how life was supposed to be. From that moment on, my normality was fractured and I became almost fearless. Mummy had died; that was *the* worst thing that could have happened to me so who cared what happened next? I think it set me on a path of independence, gave me a strength to leave school, to become a model at 16 years old, to travel the world and take every opportunity offered to me. To dive in – because what was the worst that could happen? It already had, right?

The other way of looking at the trauma of losing a parent so young is that it brings with it a sense of knowing your own mortality. That blissful bubble that most children inhabit has burst and 'it couldn't happen to me' becomes 'it *has* happened to me'.

With my mum's death came the birth of the version of me now. Does that make sense? The birth of the person whose life journey was not going to take the normal turns, but wasn't any less important or real as a result. It was a journey that would make me strong enough for what was to come; I just had to accept I would be following a different path from the one I thought was laid out for me. One thing was sure, whatever the journey, I was ready to fight for my own happy ending.

Things I Wish I Could Have Told Myself About Getting Through the Grief of Losing a Mother

1. It's going to hurt. Forever. It does get easier but the pain ebbs and flows. Some days for no apparent reason it will hit you like a train: you will be a fully grown adult talking to a relative stranger about how your mum died and completely out of the blue you will be awash with tears. Other times, when you are meant to feel it (like anniversaries or birthdays), you will feel OK. This is all completely normal and also liberating. It will make you see that she is never forgotten.

2. Be kind to yourself. By this I mean, know that sometimes you will want to go out and get drunk and forget that any of

it has happened, and that doesn't make you a bad person. It's part of the process and shouldn't be missed out. You may also sleep with people you shouldn't and that's not the end of the world either; it won't make you feel any better but use protection and don't give yourself such a hard time about it. You have to go through this stuff. It will make you stronger and shape you into the person you become.

3. Write your thoughts down; your diary is a friend. It can help put things into perspective. Remember it's your diary for your eyes only. You can write whatever you want and nobody will judge you.

4. None of this is your fault. You honestly didn't wish it or think it. It wasn't because you broke her favourite sugar bowl and never told her. It wasn't because you wrote in your diary that you hated her and wished she wasn't around. Life sucks sometimes and the only certainty is that you learn from it. But stop blaming yourself for circumstances out of your control.

5. You will dream about her throughout your life. Sometimes you will see her face so clearly it pricks the whole of your body as you sleep and other times you will be searching for her or she will be just about to open the front door or call you from the other room and when you go to find her she's not there. Her voice will fade in your memory and so will her face but in your dreams she will always be there even when you can't see her.

6. Celebrate her with those that knew her. Don't be afraid to talk about her – stories of her growing up, anecdotes of

shared dinners with friends. Keep her letters and writing, however small and insignificant. Keep her recipe books or shopping lists around the house and they will constantly surprise and comfort you when you least expect it.

7. You will forget the way she looked when she was really ill. That will not be your overriding memory of her. The brain is an amazing organ and it somehow filters out those painful memories. In all, well, *most* of your memories of your mother she will be well, I promise.

8. Don't feel guilty if you can't go to her grave or resting place regularly. It doesn't mean you don't love her or don't care. Know that she is everywhere if you look for her. This may sound really hippy dippy and hocus pocus but it's true; she's in the bright blue-sky days she loved as much as the grey, wet Sundays she hated. She's in the smell of the freesias and the warmth of a roast dinner. The wooden spoon she used daily and her favourite chair. The songs of Elaine Paige and the shelves of Marks & Spencer. You just have to look.

9. Love yourself a little bit more than you do and trust that gut instinct inside you, as it will guide you to where you are supposed to be.

10. You will always, always love her and she will always love you and that will continue forever.

Chapter 3

In the blink of an eye, I went from schoolgirl to model. I threw myself into that life wholeheartedly; I needed to get away from school and all the people who didn't know what to say to me. I wanted to change my life and concentrate on something else. Basically I needed to escape. I feel sorry for my lovely daddy and sister who had to let me go. I don't quite know what I would do or how I would feel if my daughter said to me she was going to leave school, become a model and then proceed to fly all over the world alone. I think I would probably lock her in her room and throw away the key! But my dad took it all in his stride, in the quiet way he always does.

So the story begins. One day, on the way to visiting my mum in hospital, my sister and I got 'spotted' at Bond Street tube station by a hairdresser called Tracey who was doing her final show before qualifying at Vidal Sassoon. She asked us if we would model for her and we swapped numbers and said yes. At the time I had no idea how this chance meeting would change my life.

We asked our dad and he said we could do it as it was the school holidays, so we went along to the show and had our hair put in all sorts of styles and had our make-up done as people walked around and looked at us. A modelling scout called Candida was there and afterwards said she would like to meet me. She also loved my beautiful sister, but she was only 14 and too young, so Candida and I swapped numbers and I went home to tell my dad. As I record in my diaries, he called her because he was unsure about me modelling. She obviously put his mind at rest, because a few weeks later I found myself in the offices of The Edge model agency. It was a truly surreal world; everyone seemed so grown up, even though a lot of the models were my age. They were all beautiful – tall, thin and so confident.

There I was, five foot six and reasonably pretty in a girl-next-door kind of way, but nervous as hell. Looking around me, I was completely unsure why I was there. I was measured and scrutinised and told that I had to go and test with the photographer who was an investor at the agency. He was a big deal and I was pretty scared walking into his studio. I had a white vest top on and black leggings that would become my staple wardrobe for the next few years. He sat me down and just started chatting and photographing me, putting me at ease straight away. After one roll he said he had the shot he wanted, that I had a great look and that I should think about acting and doing commercials.

At this point I have to say that it all felt like a dream. I had fallen into this mad world just by saying yes at a tube station, and now that little acting seed had been planted I could feel it growing inside me by the minute. I could do this: I could change my life, get away from school and friends who just felt sorry for me, lead a new life where I was me and no one knew about my mum being ill. I could make a living and maybe go to drama school. The world was my oyster, as my mum would have said.

Modelling was never something I really wanted to do; it was a means to an end. It was the beginning of me making decisions for myself and having little fear of the unknown. It allowed me to leave home and spread my wings at an age when most of my friends would have been terrified. It was both exhilarating and scary to take control of my destiny in such a way. You could argue that this inner strength was God-given, and it certainly manifested itself clearly with what was to come. When I decided to be a mother it was that drive and determination that saw me through the years of disappointment and then ultimately gave me the courage to see through the bumpy and sometimes thankless adoption road.

It was the late eighties when I started working and there were no such things as mobile phones or emails, so off I would go for months at a time to Paris or Tokyo, knowing nobody. My sister, my dad, my grandparents and I would write to each other constantly on those light-blue airmail paper letters that folded up to become an envelope. I have kept loads of these and it's so lovely to look back at what was happening in all of our lives then. It's funny – I never really felt lonely. I liked my own company and I loved travelling around cities and exploring new places. However, I was never really that successful as a model; my heart wasn't truly in it and, although I kept working doing all the teen magazines like *Just 17* and *Mizz*, I couldn't wait to move on to other things.

Fate intervened again at 19 years old when a film director saw me in one of these magazines and asked to meet me, so a few weeks later I met him in a hotel in London. He said he liked my look and asked if I would be interested in acting. I said yes and he gave me a few lines of his script to read. By the time I had got home there was a message for me to call my agency. The director wanted me to screen test in Paris; it was a big English/French movie and a car would be picking me up the next day.

The following morning I looked out of the window and there was a big black limo parked outside my house. I was driven in style to Heathrow airport where I boarded a plane (business class) to Paris. Arriving at the other end I was whisked off to a hotel where, once in my room, I was greeted with flowers and a bottle of champagne. I didn't have time to be scared or nervous; in a matter of hours I was in a studio on the outskirts of Paris screen testing for the part of Hélène Lagonelle in the movie *The Lover*.

The whole situation was surreal. Here I was, a normal girl from south-west London, being treated like I was a movie star. Of course I pretended that I knew exactly what I was doing and that things like this happened to me all the time.

The bravado of youth! I flew home to the news that I had got the part and I would be off to Vietnam to film for a month. During all this excitement I felt like I was leading two different lives: Lisa at home, still trying to get over my mum and going out with my school friends, and Lisa the working actress who could be anyone she wanted to be.

From that first acting job, I caught the bug. There was nothing else I wanted to do more than act and I threw myself into this new life and new opportunity. Believe me, it wasn't all as simple as my first screen test – I had a lot of disappointments and was turned down for many brilliant parts before I started actually making a name for myself. I would spend hours learning lines for different shows, deciding who that character was and dressing and acting accordingly in auditions. Then I would get knocked back and wallow in self-pity and depression before another phone call would bring the promise of a new job. And so the cycle continued.

One of the many brilliant things about being an actress was the people I would meet. Each job was all-consuming and the cast and crew would bond very quickly. It was like having a new family every few months. You would pour your heart and soul out to these people, get drunk with them and party and work as hard as you played. It was a true roller coaster of excitement and throughout my twenties my feet never really hit the ground. I had boyfriends and affairs and one-night stands, I had friends that I would party with every weekend. I had money and a car and I was living my dream.

Throughout my twenties I had quite a few boyfriends. I had been put on the pill at 17 years old by my best friend's mum, who was a doctor, as the last thing I needed was to get pregnant. I had two or three long-term boyfriends through my twenties and, despite the fact I lived with them and even got engaged a few times, babies were never really talked about. In fact I don't think they ever crossed my mind apart from knowing that one day I would have them. Being on the pill protected me from the worries of unplanned or unwanted pregnancies and I was completely and utterly caught up in my fast-paced, crazy life!

When I turned 25, my sister got pregnant. We were living together in our first flat that we had bought in North London. Her boyfriend (now husband) lived with us too. It wasn't planned and I remember her being really nervous about it. I, on the other hand, was over the moon! I couldn't believe that my little sister was going to be a mum. Though she was pretty wild in her teens, Victoria was always a bit more grown up than me, despite being two years younger. We had come to be each other's mother in so many ways and now she was going to be a mummy for real.

Talking to my sis about this time now, she said that I was away a lot. By then I had got a part in *Brookside* and I was filming in Liverpool, so I wasn't there for her a lot of the time. She said that it was very different to now, and that she went alone to some weird NCT class to which no husbands or partners were invited. I do remember that I would come home from work and talk and sing to her bump and when she asked me if I would be her birth partner (along with her Allen, of course) I jumped at the chance. I was so honoured that she had asked me to be at the birth of her baby. What's funny is that motherhood wasn't even on my radar at this point. I was super happy for my sister but it never even crossed my mind to think about it happening to me. I have asked my sister a number of times over the years about this; I've been so sure that her pregnancy must have started my biological clock ticking, but no, apparently not in the least!

I was up in Liverpool filming when I got the call from Victoria to say that her waters had broken and that I needed to get down there. I had obviously briefed the production crew and asked that, if at all possible, I would like to have the time off. As soon as I got the call, they cut me out of the scene I was shooting so that I could leave straight away. I remember my heart banging in my chest and butterflies flapping in my stomach as I made my way to the train station. I had no real idea of what to expect and I just wanted to be there for my sister but there was a four-hour train journey between us. After I boarded the train, a man sat across the table from me and asked me if I was all right. It's funny that, even though I am an actress, whenever something is happening to me in real life, good or bad, my face can't seem to hide it. I told him that my sister was about to give birth and I was her birth partner and he went to the bar and bought me a vodka and tonic to steady my nerves. Looking back, I think he may have plied me with vodka the whole train journey, as it passed in a flash with him keeping me talking all the time. Luckily I made it to London in one piece, albeit a little squiffy!

I went straight to the hospital, sweeping in and giving my sister a big hug. My dad was already there and Allen was pacing about a bit and looking nervous. I needn't have worried about making it in time for the birth: my sister's labour took hours and we were by the bed telling stories and remembering anecdotes from our childhood well into the night before any pushing started.

I remember how it seemed that one minute there were three of us in the room along with the midwife: Victoria, Allen and me. Allen and I were both whispering words of encouragement and rubbing my sister's back or squeezing her hands and then – whoosh – there was a scream and silence and then a sort of animal mewing and baaing as my beautiful niece entered the world. The three of us became four and our world was never the same again.

I feel very blessed to have witnessed the birth of another human being. It really is a miracle. The excitement of not knowing whether my sister was having a boy or a girl and the surprise when she came out. The calmness of a newborn, the quiet stillness that descends on the room. It's all magic. Allen cut the umbilical cord, a strong proper London geezer reduced to tears as he kissed his daughter. Exhausted but smiling, my sister looked truly beautiful and about 12 years old.

And suddenly the little bundle was being passed to me. Lola ... so tiny and light in my arms, still covered in goo with a tiny pink face and proper rosebud lips. Lola made me feel like I suddenly had a purpose. I never knew the love I could feel for a human being until that moment. I knew I would do anything for this child, this new addition to our family. I have a photo of me meeting Lola and my face is full of wonder at this tiny miracle. I was going to love and protect her forever … but did I want a baby for myself yet? Had my womb started calling? No way!

I will always be so very grateful to my sister for including me so much in Lola's entrance into the world and life ever after. Though she admits now that she had all the new mums' fears of someone dropping her baby, she let me look after Lola all the time, teaching me how to change her nappy and how to feed her. She taught me how to wind her, how to watch for signs that she was pooing or hungry or tired. Together we rocked her and sang to her and showered her with love. She was like a brilliant dolly to me and I bought her more clothes than she could possibly wear. My sister and godmother still laugh now about the completely impractical but beautiful pure silk dresses I bought her! I should mention here that my sister just seemed to know what to do. It was like motherhood was already programmed into her. She was and still is my hero, the mother I want to be, the mother that I learned so much from and the mother I still always turn to, whether for advice on Billie or advice for me.

A few months after Lola was born, I landed a part in a brand-new TV series called *Holby City*. It was here I met my two best friends Angela and Nicola. From the minute I met Ange and Nic we were inseparable. We were invited to a big do in London, all so excited to be working together, and we met up in the ladies' loos and sat in there all night just chatting and chatting. We swapped phone numbers and I remember both of them calling the next day and me thinking that this was it, besties forever. I think you could probably describe our friendship as a love affair. We had boyfriends but we didn't really need them; all we needed was each other. We were all at the cusp of our careers, invited to every showbiz party in London. And we were going to embrace it. We laughed constantly, went away on holidays together, read the same books, made each other dinners and hangover breakfasts, did spells on boys, stayed up all night, cried and confided in each other. Those two girls set the scene for the circle of strong women that would always be in my life. They were a support network, just like my mum's group of friends, entwined forever. None of us thought about babies.

Three years later, my second niece Eva Rose came along. Ange and I were out partying when I got the phone call saying that Victoria's waters had broken and to come quickly. I rushed to the hospital in a taxi wearing a huge jumper and jeans, walked into my sister's room and she took one look at me and said, 'You're pissed!' I tried to style it out but, within minutes of being in that hot, airless hospital, the room started spinning and Victoria had to give me her big T-shirt that she had set aside to give birth in. She wasn't too happy with me and it sobered me up fast!

The birth of Eva Rose was much faster than Lola and seemed even more calm and easy. She arrived looking big and bouncing, with a shock of dark hair and the cutest little round face and button nose. There's something about the smell of babies that makes everything feel OK with the world and Eva certainly had that effect on me. Staring down at this bundle in my arms I fell in love a second time and vowed to always be there for her. At this time in my life I was seeing someone I had really fallen for and I remember feeling the first stirring of something. That maybe I wasn't quite ready for this yet but it wasn't far off. A definite flutter of something in my womb, a definite maybe of wanting ... but just not quite yet.

Another guy I had been dating was adamant that he wanted children, not just his own birth children but to adopt too, and how did I feel about that? I remember nodding and smiling along and making all the right noises but in reality I couldn't see that path for me. I wasn't at all sure that I could properly love a child that I hadn't made myself. So many responsibilities and potential difficulties seemed to come with it. But I was still young and carefree, so I put it out of my mind. Oh, the twists and turns of life!

My oldest best friend Emma was the first of my friends to have a baby. Emma and I met on my first day of secondary school. We had both had a pretty hard time at our previous schools being bullied and we got on like a house on fire. She is the only friend that knew me before and after my mum died. We are like family. When my mum was ill, Emma promised her that she would always look after me and be there for me, something I never knew until years later, and she has certainly kept to her word.

Emma had her first baby Evie, my goddaughter, when I was 30. I remember going to see her in hospital the day she was born. It was a cold, wet Boxing Day and, when I got to the hospital, Emma was sitting in a chair holding her new baby. She looked beautiful and serene and exhausted all at the same time. I remember thinking that this was it now, we were all on that baby roller coaster and that glow of believing that it would all happen to me at some point was a lovely feeling.

About a year later I met my (now ex) husband, Chris. We were working together and we fell in love. I was 30 years old and at this point in my life I was ready to settle down. We were together 24/7 and after about six months we decided to move in and a little later buy a house together. It was at this point that my biological clock started ticking and it went from a soft tick to a disco beat pretty damn fast! We decided that we would try to have a baby so I came off the pill. It was so exciting to have made that decision, to think that I had met the man I wanted to have children with. Those first few months of trying were bliss. It felt like we had a little secret that the rest of the world didn't know about. I envisaged the pair of us telling our families our good news, me getting fatter and blooming, holding a baby in my arms … it all felt within touching distance and life was good.

A few months after we had started 'trying', my best friend Ange found out that she was pregnant. She hadn't been seeing her boyfriend for very long but they were so happy together and were over the moon that this had happened purely by accident. I remember her telling me; she was nervous and scared but clearly excited and I was thrilled for her. However, I have to say that this was the very first time that the pregnancy jealousy monster hit me. I could feel this thing rising up from my stomach. I was so genuinely pleased for her, but I had been trying and I hadn't got pregnant yet and she had just come along and done it without even intending to. It stirred my soul and made me even more determined that we were going to be next. I started cutting down on my alcohol intake and thinking a little more seriously about my diet, not to the extent that anyone would know, but just for me.

I think at this point I maybe started to feel a little impatient about things, but it was more of a niggle than a fully fledged feeling. It hadn't even crossed my mind that my partner would have to change his diet or lifestyle (that came much later!). I think, as we had moved into our first grown-up home, I was definitely feeling the pull of adult life and was happy to slow down my partying, instead swapping it for cosy nights in, making dinner. But our relationship was still relatively shiny and new, so it felt exciting, as if we were moving on to the next level.

Five months later, on Valentine's Day morning, I was lying in bed and it occurred to me that my period was late. I had been so busy filming a new series that I hadn't noticed. Chris was away filming and I was travelling to Manchester that day to see him. I was lying alone, butterflies starting to swirl in my stomach at the prospect of what today might hold. I was up and dressed in the blink of an eye and practically ran to the chemist to pick up a pregnancy test. I bought two, just in case. I hurried home with a thumping heart and a full bladder and waited for the stick to tell my fortune. Two blue lines appeared, the second one fainter than the first but there was definitely a line. *Two* lines ... I was pregnant.

I rushed to get ready to board a train to Manchester. On the journey I went to the loo again and did another test just to make sure. Two lines. Still there. I called my sister from the train toilet and told her my news. I was beside myself with excitement. A grin from ear to ear. She was so happy for me but I told her not to tell anyone. I then texted Chris. 'Happy Valentine's Day, Daddy!' He came running to meet me at the station and I handed him the test. He was as excited and happy as I was.

Holding on to our secret, Chris and I spent the weekend in a blur. I was going to have a baby. I could almost immediately feel my body changing. I felt unbelievably exhausted and just so very happy. I had joined the club!

A few days later I was at work, filming. It was snowing and freezing and I just wasn't feeling quite right. I felt sick and I had pains in my abdomen. I had told my co-star (already a mother) the day before and we were basking in my happy news. I mentioned to her that I felt pains and she said that she thought it was probably quite normal.

Later that day, I was filming a scene and I had the worst cramping and pain on one side of my tummy. One minute

I was standing on set saying my lines and the next I had collapsed on the floor. I was taken to my dressing room where the medic came to see me. I told him that I was pregnant and I remember him looking at me strangely, asking if I had any pain in my shoulder (a tell-tale sign of ectopics). I didn't. He said that I needed to get to the hospital straight away, as something wasn't right. I kept saying, 'But it will be OK, won't it?' and he wouldn't quite meet my eye.

I was driven to hospital, where I was examined by the doctor. A nurse took my bloods and gave me another pregnancy test, which confirmed I was pregnant. I then just lay on a bed for hours, waiting for the blood test results to come through, praying that everything would be all right. I was in so much pain.

Eventually, I had an ultrasound, which confirmed that my pregnancy was ectopic. I had never heard this word before and nobody really explained it to me. I kept saying to the nurse, 'But does that mean I'm still pregnant? Can I still have the baby?' I was in complete shock. Eventually a kind nurse sat with me and explained what an ectopic pregnancy was. She told me that the foetus was growing in the fallopian tube and not in my womb. My egg had fertilised in the wrong place and therefore it could never be a viable pregnancy. I still couldn't really get my head around this information. Surely in this day and age they could move it to the right place? Surely this wasn't the end?

Within minutes of having the ultrasound I had another severe burst of pain. A very officious young doctor came into the room at that moment and asked me some questions, seemingly completely devoid of any feeling for my situation. It was 18 February, the day before my 32nd birthday, and when I told him this, his advice was not to have any cake as they would be operating and removing the foetus immediately. My world fell to pieces. I remember looking at Chris and him saying it was all going to be OK and then I blacked out.

When I came round I was lying in a bed in a small hospital room. I was linked up to a drip and Chris and my dad and my sister were there, all looking at me with the saddest eyes. All hope was gone. My baby was no more.

Those few days in hospital were just awful. I cried and slept and took more morphine and cried some more. Chris was completely overwhelmed by grief, too. In a matter of a week our lives had gone from the two of us to three and back to two again, with a huge gap left in between us where the pregnancy once was.

It was only early days and yet it didn't stop me from feeling such a wave of grief. Such loss for something I had wanted so desperately. The surgeon who operated on me told me that he had had to remove the tube as it had ruptured, which is why I was in so much pain. But he went on to say that the other tube was fine and he could see no reason why I wouldn't go on to have a successful pregnancy. He was a really lovely man, unlike the doctor I had seen previously, but he spoke in doctor talk and I didn't feel like he or anybody else understood what I had gone through.

The other factor that didn't help things was that I was on a gynae ward right next to maternity, and all around me there were lots of women with big bumps being kept in for observation. At the time I hated all of them. At least they had the decency to put me in a private room, away from them all. My best friend Ange came to visit me, glowing from her own pregnancy, and I just broke down and cried. Why couldn't that be me?

These days were dark, dark times. I wallowed in my pain and sadness for weeks. In the days that followed, people kept telling me that it was all right, that it was only the early stages of pregnancy and that I could get pregnant again. But it wasn't a small thing to me. I always feel for the people who have miscarriages in the first few weeks of their pregnancy, as they are placated with the same comments. I think when you get that primal urge for a baby and you find out you are pregnant, your brain goes into overdrive. You become attached to your pregnancy, to your growing baby so very quickly and days can feel like months. It's never just a little thing, however early it is.

When I was recuperating at home, my friend Emma came over to look after me. She lived on the other side of London and bundled her baby Evie and her husband Dan into the car and they cooked us Sunday lunch and Emma tidied the house. I was a shell, sitting on the sofa, not even able to interact with my beautiful goddaughter. Just looking at her reminded me of the failure I was. I couldn't even grow a baby in the right place. Although I was a mess and my friends all had their own lives going on and new babies, they all rallied round, cooking, sending self-help books, dropping in for cups of tea and hugs. Throughout that time I felt so loved and looked after by my friends and family and I know that, without that network of people behind me, I may not have got through it.

I became fixated on getting better and trying again for a baby. I started back at work and began looking for things to take my mind off what had happened. With perfect timing, Chris proposed to me, and it gave me a new lease of life, something to think about and plan and look forward to. I have to say that us getting married – a stage that should have been joyous togetherness, the two of us embarking on a new journey – was just what I needed. But if I'm really honest, I'm not sure I was consistently and entirely present during the planning of the big day. I loved it all but there was always that slight feeling of mania hanging over me, that desperate wanting. A wedding was the perfect distraction. We were very happy and very much in love and, for a few months, that tided me over. It should have been enough, but in my mind I was already onto the next thing. I was trying to speed up the healing process and the ticking biological clock was now deafening.

I had been told by the doctor that if after a year of trying nothing had happened, then we could look at other options. The first thing to do would be to try a few months on Clomid, a drug that stimulates your ovaries and was getting very good results.

All I could think was there was no way I was waiting a year; that was an impossible amount of time. I decided I would give it six months, which would take us to just after the wedding, and then I would see the doctor again to start trying the Clomid.

Looking back, I can see that, as soon as I was out of hospital and feeling well enough, life for us as a couple definitely changed, though I am not sure Chris was even aware of it. To be fair to him, he just went along with my plans because he thought it would make me happy. I had another chance. If I failed to get pregnant naturally after six months, I could do it with the help of Clomid. One way or another I was sure we would conceive, albeit my chances were halved because I only had one tube.

I read up on how to maximise my chances of conception and threw myself into eating healthily and trying to cut down on alcohol. I went to yoga religiously to de-stress and to keep my body flexible and fit without going to the gym and pounding my body on the treadmill or bike, as that was bad for fertility apparently. I read somewhere that pineapple was great for increasing sperm count and it became a staple in our fridge.

I loved that I could wee on a stick and I would actually get the line I wanted to see when I was fertile, my body surprising me by doing exactly what it was actually meant to do. Every time this happened, it fed the much-needed hope that things would work out and I would get pregnant. Sex definitely became regimented almost immediately after the ectopic, but it was also fun. I had a new lease of life, a reason for getting up in the morning.

I can't honestly remember how long it was fun for before it became a chore, the only reason for doing it being to conceive. I don't think it was that long. Once those hormones take hold, you have little control over them. I see now that this would have put unnecessary strain on our relationship, but at the time I was suffering from a bad case of biological clock-ticking blindness. In the early days I was good at disguising this and dressing up our efforts to get pregnant as fun, inventive, romantic shagging, but the edge in my voice and behaviour was definitely starting to show. It was especially worse when, every month, I was greeted by my super-reliable, four-weeks-to-the-day, ever-faithful period.

By the time it came to planning my wedding, I had a new spike of energy and could disguise my angst and longing again. I began hoping that fate would be as romantic as I felt and give me the pregnancy I so desperately wanted. I had six months to plan the big day and six months to conceive naturally. I constantly daydreamed that I would have to make a last-minute phone call to my wedding dress maker, fantasising about telling her that she needed to add some fabric to my dress because I was starting to show. In fact, I had many dress fittings and the size of my bust would fluctuate wildly depending on whereabouts in my cycle I was at the time of the fitting. Another spectacular reminder that my body was doing everything right on the outside but somewhere inside me it was all going wrong.

I have to say, though, that planning my wedding did keep me going. I loved the roller coaster of it all, Chris and I were very happy and the romantic inside me remained convinced that at some point between now and then, or at the very least on my honeymoon, I would conceive. Life felt pretty damn good again and I was smiling and positive. I was probably slightly more giddy at the prospect of trying for a baby than the marriage itself, or maybe it was equal measures. The excitement of the wedding preparation felt like a great healer, and for a while it was, but as the heat on our non-stop trying increased, the sticking plaster was definitely peeling at the edges. Again, this is something I can only now see retrospectively.

All my close friends and family knew what I was going through by this time, but they stopped asking too many questions. I was just focused on staying positive that it would happen for us – that there were either going to be three of us on our wedding day, or three of us very soon after. As I look back I remember feeling upbeat, despite all the setbacks. The prospect of starting on Clomid after the wedding gave me new focus and optimism. The world was a shiny place full of hope again.

A pregnancy would be the answer to my prayers. The chances of conceiving on Clomid were very high; the only worry was that we might end up with twins, if my ovaries were over-stimulated. That wouldn't be a problem – that would be a miracle! Already my heart had started beating again and all we had to do was have sex. A lot. I could feel it; the wanting was nearly over.

Eventually the big day came round and the wedding was wonderful, a fabulous day where we were surrounded by our family and friends. I couldn't help but get caught up in all the excitement. But once it was over, reality hit me: I still wasn't pregnant and that was the only thing that mattered.

Steak and béarnaise sauce

At a time in my life where I wanted everything to be perfect, I would make steak and homemade chips and béarnaise sauce every Friday night. It would steady me and make me feel I had a little control and that we were a normal couple and that the sun would shine for us again.

2 ribeye steaks weighing about 220g each
Olive oil
Salt and pepper
For the béarnaise
100ml white wine vinegar
1 shallot chopped
A few sprigs of tarragon
2 egg yolks
125g melted butter

To make the sauce, put the vinegar, shallot and tarragon into a small saucepan and bring to the boil. Cook until reduced by about ¾. Leave to cool and pour into a large pyrex bowl.

Place the bowl over a pan of simmering water (make sure the base of the bowl does not touch the water). Add the yolks and whisk until you can see the whisk leaving a pattern in the sauce. Take the bowl off the heat and whisk in the melted butter little by little, keep whisking until all the butter is used or your arm has fallen off! Season to taste.

For the steaks
Preheat a fry or griddle pan over a high heat. Season the steaks and rub all over with olive oil. Cook the steaks in the very hot pan for approx. 2–3 minutes each side depending on whether you like your steak rare or medium. Turn off the heat and turn the steaks again and leave in the pan for about 3–4 minutes to rest.

Serve with homemade (or bought) chips, a big dollop of the béarnaise and a lovely glass of wine!

Chapter 4

I think I'm a pretty good person. I work hard, I think about others, I try to always be kind. If I put my mind to something and focus then I usually get it … so why was it proving so difficult for me to get pregnant? After all, this was something that millions of women do every day, very easily and without even thinking, sometimes without even wanting it. As I read back over these few lines it all seems quite glaringly obvious. Getting pregnant isn't just a spreadsheet of boxes you can tick. Yes, eating well and not drinking booze and having lots of sex at the right time should just about cover it, but maybe pregnancy is a bit like trying to make meringue on a stormy day … temperamental. Maybe your womb hears and feels your longing and perhaps that desperation, somehow, repulses it?

Certainly it seems the more you want and work at it, the less likely you are to get it, which just made no sense to me at all. So many well-meaning people said to me: 'You just need to *relax* and it will happen.' But that was the problem, I couldn't relax. How could I when my body wouldn't do what I needed it to? No matter how hard I tried or how big an act I put on, I was as tense and as wound up as a coiled spring, obsessing over every fluctuation of my monthly cycle. I was frantic.

I have to ask myself here, why did I feel that way? How deep was the longing? Was I devastated because my baby had gone, or was it that my perfect scenario had hit a bump in the road? Was it like that time I became obsessed over a boy at school? I wanted him and did everything in my power to get him, only to realise that, when the prize was finally mine, I didn't actually want him anymore. Was I simply part of the 'if I want it then I should have it immediately' generation? I can't deny that there probably was a very small part of me that got hooked on the chase. That the more impossible it seemed, the more the 'dog with the bone' inside me said *that's not going to stop me.*

It could have been all of those things, but I also know it was deeper than that. I wanted to grow a baby. I wanted to feel all the things I had started to feel when life threw me the ectopic. I wanted someone to love unconditionally, to nurture and mould and show the way, someone to watch grow and flourish. I wanted to be the hand to hold, the person they would run to. I was desperate to be a mother with all of my heart and at any cost.

I felt at the time that not being a mother would make me invisible, because fundamentally, what was the next stage of my life going to be without children? Everywhere I looked, people were pregnant or wheeling buggies and carrying babies; how on earth was I going to navigate my thirties when all of my social circle was in this child-rearing bubble? If I wasn't to be a mother then what was I? What was my reason for being here?

I had plenty of reasons to feel good about myself. I had a fantastic career that I had carved out for myself, by myself. I was strong and fiercely independent. But this wasn't enough for me. I didn't want to be looked upon as the 'career woman' who had put work before having a family, though lots of well-meaning relatives had started to say that in a clumsy attempt to make me feel better. It didn't make me feel better as it wasn't what I wanted. Also, all I could think was, why should I have to choose? Was there actually a choice in the first place? Why couldn't I have both? Plenty of my friends and peers were successful actresses *and* mothers.

I know when most people think of 'career women', they classically think of a hardened, tough-talking woman, in a suit, with very expensive handbags, always jetting off alone on city breaks and wearing designer clothes, living a selfish life and having no desire for a child. But that wasn't me. I had a great career, yes, but without a baby, there was no softness and a shedload of loneliness in my life.

There were no books or films that showed me an alternative route, either. Even my idol, Carrie Bradshaw, hadn't yet decided that she wasn't going to be a mother. She was safely ensconced with Aiden, thinking about Big, but her jury was definitely still out, and the sequels hadn't yet been made. The truth is that no one ever told me that I could have a life (and a very fulfilling one) without kids. My mum wasn't around to talk this through with me, and there was no counter argument wherever I looked.

I think now that things are very different (*SATC* proves my point!). I have read books recently that, had they been around at that time of my life, might have empowered me to embrace my childlessness and find another way. Many women are of course completely fulfilled without being mothers – some actively and honestly choose to ignore that path, even if it is open to them. Equally, many women are mothers and are actually unfulfilled. Motherhood doesn't need to define you if you don't want it to. But I wanted it to. There definitely wasn't another option for me.

Chris and I were at the start of our marriage and everything should have been rosy. We should have been walking around in that newlywed Meghan and Harry glow, having sex anywhere and everywhere, completely caught up in each other. To some extent, we were all of those things, but my desire for a baby since my ectopic had escalated. It was as if my longing for a baby had started to block out all of the light. The pin in the grenade had definitely been taken out and in my head all hell had broken loose. Time was ticking ... I needed my baby and I needed it now. Already the spontaneity had been stripped out of our relationship and we were on that fertility treadmill. All hands on deck and no room for any kind of relaxed approach, which didn't exactly allow us to exist in the newlywed bubble.

The first step on the assisted fertility roundabout was getting us both tested at the doctors. All our bloods and sperm count had come back as normal so the doctor officially started us on Clomid. I was 33 years old at this point and I wasn't getting any younger; all I could hear when I closed my eyes was that tick tock of my biological clock. I felt like I was Alice in Wonderland following the White Rabbit down a rabbit hole and constantly worrying that I was too late. I only had one fallopian tube, so my chances of conceiving each month had been halved. I felt as if I was getting older by the minute – I needed this to happen quick smart! The panic and anxiety truly set in once the wedding was over and I waited for this magical drug to answer my prayers.

So before I knew it, there I was, popping my first Clomid tablet. For those who are lucky enough not to know the drill, you take the drug for four days a month, usually between days two and five of your cycle. It is a tiny little tablet – it looks utterly harmless. Even vitamin tablets are bigger. As I filled a glass of water and popped the tablet onto my tongue, I asked myself: 'What can this minuscule tablet really do to me?'

In reality that tiny, innocuous-looking pill completely changed everything about me. My mood instantly switched and, within two hours of taking it, I became a total monster. I was irritable and angry and the last thing on my mind was having sex, which seemed to me a fundamental flaw in the Clomid plan.

I remember lying on my bathroom floor in a pool of tears after just one day of taking it, crying that I hadn't managed to get pregnant again, crying that life seemed so unfair, and a few minutes later feeling totally fine and bleaching all the sinks and washing all the floors and writing lists of what needed doing.

True mania! I spent a lot of time in my local chemist at that point in my life, buying fertility sticks so that I knew when I was perfectly fertile and could have regimented sex. I would text or call Chris and tell him to get home immediately. When he came in, I would run upstairs and tell him, 'Right, it's time.' No time for foreplay or to make each other feel wanted, just 'Quick! Come on!' Afterwards I would lie for hours with my legs in the air, praying to the fertility gods and Buddhas I had around my home.

At first, as I have said, it was fun: a quickie on the kitchen floor, both of us excitedly thinking this could be the time we would get pregnant. But after a while of sex on demand, as much as I don't want to admit it, the fun did slowly disappear. You're not doing it because you desperately desire each other; you're doing it for one thing only. That feeling of failure every month as my period arrived was almost unbearable, and I alternated between being angry at myself and angry at my husband. Whose fault was this? Always a little voice in my head telling me it was mine, that my body didn't work, that I wasn't good enough.

When I think back to the pressure I put us under, I marvel at the fact we didn't implode much earlier. My husband was living with a complete stranger, who veered between being angry and screaming the house down one minute, to crying in a heap on the floor and then demanding that he get home from football because the fertility stick said we had to get to it. At the time I couldn't see it from his perspective, I only thought he wanted the same as me. I now see the selfishness of it all. I don't think I ever actually asked; I just assumed that he was on the same ride and, to a huge extent, he was. But looking back I now realise that he had a shedload of patience for a crazy new wife who couldn't conceive. More importantly, a wife who acted nothing like the woman he had married.

Everywhere I went – parties, baby showers (and there suddenly seemed to be a load of them), dinners with friends, even the supermarket – I would get talking to people about my lack of baby. Friends of friends would tell me that they had a friend in the same position and that they had seen someone amazing and they had suddenly got pregnant. I would run home with this shiny new nugget of information and think: 'This will be the thing that will work for me' – I clung on to anything and everything. One such 'nugget' was a man in London who had great success in getting women pregnant. I was given a phone number on a scrap of paper and told to make an appointment. I called and a heavily accented woman answered the phone, she was very kind and listened to my story and told me that, yes, her husband could help me.

I made an appointment as soon as I could and travelled by tube to his address. I arrived at a rather tired-looking but grand apartment block and climbed three flights of stairs to the front door. It was opened by a very glamorous woman with jet-black hair tied back in a bun. She looked like a cross between a headmistress and a stern nurse, but when she smiled it changed her whole face. She told me I had come to the right place and took me down a dark corridor, which seemed to have loads of little rooms leading off. Most of the doors were shut. I was told

LISA FAULKNER

to sit on the bed in a room that looked like it had once been a nursery, and wait. The walls were a little damp with peeling wallpaper and the curtains slightly threadbare. The situation felt very strange but I honestly didn't care. I was excited.

Eventually, after what seemed like hours, a man came into the room. He had a big smile and, I can't be sure, but what looked like a toupee on his head. He told me to lie down and take off my shoes and socks. He then produced what appeared to be a toothbrush from his pocket. He took my feet in his hand and started pressing certain points and then sort of 'digging' into the pad of my big toe with the end of the toothbrush. 'Owww!' I screamed. 'Yes,' he said, 'it is your pituitary gland that is blocked and that is why you are not getting pregnant. I need to change the energy and then you will be fine.'

After about five to ten minutes of prodding and digging on my feet he said that he wanted to see me again the following week. He then suddenly leaned forward, gave me a kiss, and left the room. As I was putting on my shoes and socks, I could hear a woman in the next room making bizarre moaning and groaning sounds. She was no doubt having her feet seen to as well. I paid the lovely lady and left.

I went back about three or four times to the strange flat with the obscure smiley man with the toothbrush, who would always insist on giving me a kiss at the end of the session. I have to say, I didn't really know what to make of the whole situation and I certainly didn't feel comfortable with any of it. But believe me, when you're on the mission that I was, you don't really think too much about things, you just go along in the blind hope that it will work. It was all very surreal, and after a few weeks of hearing the strange noises coming from the other bedrooms and enduring the weird kissing scenario, I decided it wasn't for me – and, more importantly, it wasn't working. I didn't go back, but I was more determined than ever that there had to be another way.

At one of the many baby showers I went to, I got talking to a heavily pregnant woman who said that hypnotherapy had worked for her. She said that sometimes, something in your past is blocking you from conceiving and that stress is a big factor in preventing conception. The idea is that your patterns of behaviour can be changed while you are 'under'. This really struck a chord with me at that time, as I was definitely aware that my thoughts were super negative and that maybe this was all part of the problem. I went home clutching another phone number, a new nugget, a new hope.

Again, I traipsed into town, to a woman who had all the right credentials. She told me how hypnotherapy worked and led me into a small green room with a comfy sofa. I sat down and she started talking me through a relaxation exercise. I remember feeling sleepy and then regressing 15 years and talking about my mum and crying and crying. I couldn't stop. The woman took me out of the 'state' I was in and brought me back to reality but I was still crying and it wasn't letting up. I am not sure she knew what to do with me and she kept looking at the clock, as our session was very nearly up. She told me she was going to try to take me back again so that I would stop crying.

She wasn't particularly friendly or warm and by this point all I knew was that I just wanted to get out of there. I let her talk me through her relaxation steps again, all the while singing Kylie Minogue's 'I Should Be So Lucky' in my head, so that I wouldn't be properly present. I managed to stop myself from crying at the bizarreness of the situation and, once I was 'back in the room', she told me that I was going to need a lot of sessions to get me through my obviously raw grief before I could even think about getting pregnant.

Here I have to say that I'm sure hypnotherapy has worked for a lot of people. I am not knocking it and I am sure there is a large amount of truth in what she said. However, I had spent years in therapy after my mum died and, although I was far from 'over' her death (something I don't think you ever achieve, you just learn to live with it), I was definitely in a more settled place and had dealt with a lot of the pain and loss. I didn't feel I needed to be regressed quite that far, and plunged back into the pain and shock of her immediate death. And, more to the point, loads of people I knew had been through similar grief and turmoil and it hadn't stopped them from getting pregnant. The other matter was time: I simply didn't have time to go through all the therapy sessions that she said I needed! I left and never returned, though I did cry for several days afterwards. Whether that was the effect of the hypnotherapy, the Clomid or the sheer upset of 'the wanting', I will never know.

A little while later I was asked to appear on *This Morning* to talk about a show I had coming out. The lovely Fern Britton was presenting at the time and I adored her. We had met before on *This Morning* and *Ready Steady Cook* and she had always been so kind and lovely to me. In the break I told her of my sadness and loss and longing for a baby and she told me that a woman called Zita West was on the show to talk about fertility. She was an expert in the field and would be very happy to talk to me. Fern told me to go to her dressing room where we wouldn't be disturbed and she would get Zita to come and talk to me.

Zita was lovely, warm and kind and had heard stories like mine over and over. She gave me her card and asked me to come to her office, telling me I needed proper support and to talk through all the available options. I thanked both her and Fern from the bottom of my heart. I have never forgotten that act of kindness from someone I didn't know very well. Fern had seen I was obviously in distress and had wanted to help. I remember feeling pretty overwhelmed that someone had taken an interest and felt my pain.

I made an appointment to see Zita and she put Chris and me on a course of vitamin supplements that were meant to help us conceive. Everything was taken into consideration – our lifestyles, diet, age – and then a plan was tailor-made for us. Again, I returned home full of hope. We dutifully took our vitamins and I started back at yoga, which made me feel at least a little more human. Zita wanted me to see her hypnotherapist and, although I was pretty scared after my last experience, I did as I was told. This session was a million times better than the other person I had seen; I didn't have to sing any Kylie to get through it. The therapist gave me lots of tools and visualisations to put me in a more relaxed state and ease my everyday stress. I have used those techniques at times over the years and they still work. In fact I did one on Billie a few years ago and whenever she can't get to sleep we do the visualisation together.

During all this time Chris never really complained about taking the vitamins or having his life turned upside down. He didn't get irritated or express any concern at my behaviour. I think when you're completely immersed in it, you can't see what's actually happening right before your eyes and I was blinded by anything but my need for this baby. So, weirdly, I was actually quite happy to come off the Clomid. I felt very businesslike about it – as far as I was concerned it hadn't fulfilled its promise in any way, so that was that, we needed to move on.

I was meant to do a course of three months, then have a break, and then do another three months, and I carried the next prescription around in my bag for ages. I made an appointment to see my doctor and she told me to give myself a break. Clearly, the Clomid wasn't working and I obviously wasn't dealing with the physical and mental side effects at all well. She recommended that I went to see a counsellor who was trained in CBT (cognitive behavioural therapy). CBT helps you see patterns in your behaviour and gives you tools to help to change your negative thoughts or way of thinking. It's meant to be great therapy in dealing with stress and grief.

The mind is a very powerful thing and, unfortunately, I let mine rule me, not the other way round. I went to see a CBT therapist and we sat and talked through why I was there. Therapy is fantastic when it works, but you have to gel with the therapist and feel some sort of emotional connection, otherwise it's just time wasted and £50 down the drain each week. I felt no connection with the therapist and when they suggested I start keeping a diary of my behaviour, so that I could take control of my situation, I felt deflated and tired. I didn't want to help myself at that time, or more importantly, I didn't feel like I needed help at the time. I knew the cure for me and that was a baby. I wasn't mad; I just needed to get pregnant. I never went back to the therapist and, for a while, I didn't see my doctor because I felt too scared of explaining why I stopped going.

So I was left with a prescription for more Clomid and not much else. Clomid was meant to be the Holy Grail, the halfway house between natural and aided conception, but it had failed me. I felt a huge sense of disappointment at the failure of that little pill and terrified that what was next for me was IVF. That was massive. I felt like I was standing in the middle of a merry-go-round and that, every time I tried something, it failed and went spinning out of my hands. All I was left with was a feeling of blinding dizziness.

After a further few months of trying – we were *always* trying – we were still nowhere. I felt so desperate in every way. Sad and lost and praying for a miracle. I think it's also important to say here that I had lost all sense of time and that my perception of time was severely warped. A few months seemed like years. I'm not pointing the finger or trying to blame anyone, but at no point did anybody say to me, 'STOP!' No doctors told me that I should maybe slow down, that my body had been through a lot of trauma. Even my family and friends didn't intervene. Why was that? Was it because the force of 'me' is completely unstoppable when it wants to be? Would I have stuck my fingers in my ears and told them to shut up if they had? I felt like I was trapped in this spider's web, hurtling along on a journey that felt interminable when, in reality, it was actually less than two years. That really isn't that long in the grand scheme of things.

I sometimes wonder what would have happened if I had just stopped right there and then. If I had found my calm place and made peace with my situation, would the clock have stopped ticking? Would I have let it? Just remembering this fills my head with the terrifyingly familiar noise and madness. That chaos all comes instantly flooding back and highlights that, actually, what I needed most at that time was a bit of silence. I didn't give myself a chance to heal or reflect, I just ploughed on in the only way I knew how, full of desperation, obsession, impatience and irrationality.

After another meeting with Zita she suggested I go and see a man called Dr Taranissi at the ARGC clinic (the Assisted Reproduction and Gynaecology Centre). He was the best IVF doctor around and had a ridiculously high success rate. She definitely didn't push the IVF idea, she just gently nudged and said that it would be good to see him and explore it as an option. There was a procedure called IUI, which we could definitely try before having IVF, but, whatever I did first, I was told that he was definitely the person to go to.

It's funny because I write in my diary at the time that I thought of IVF as the last resort. I never dreamed that I would end up there because, essentially, my body was in full working order. I'd had all the tests so IVF, if we got to that stage, was a no brainer. Wasn't it? I had read about IVF, about the process and, I have to say, it didn't faze me at all. In fact it felt like it was part of my destiny; the reason I had actually taken the time to read magazine articles and research it was because this was meant to be the next stage in my journey.

Yes, I felt that my body had let me down, that I had let myself down, but the actual process of IVF seemed relatively easy if you were young and healthy. I had heard that it was quite invasive and that there were injections involved, but I didn't really ask myself what that meant. I remember reading a book about a woman in her forties who was going through IVF; she regaled the reader with funny stories about her mad behaviour, the pain of the injections and injecting yourself in weird and inappropriate places, of all sense of dignity lost as yet another stranger examined your most private parts, and I smiled and thought: 'Yes, but that won't be me, I'm nowhere near 40, nowhere near that crazy, nowhere near that frazzled.' I had the blindness of youth and complete belief that IVF would work for me. I admit now that I even felt that I was a slight IVF imposter – that there really was still a chance I could conceive naturally and I was just speeding up the process. Oh, how little I knew!

Hindsight is a wonderful thing and I see now as I look back that my husband would never know who he was getting when the front door opened. He had met and married a fun-loving, carefree party girl, someone who loved going out and being with people, always fun, always up for a laugh, who cooked a bit and drunk a lot. In the space of 18 months I had turned into someone unrecognisable. I didn't want to party any more; I didn't want to drink at all unless it was a glass of wine on the sofa. I turned into a homemaker, always cleaning and cooking and baking, trying to take my mind off things, achingly ready for the next stage of my life. I do think a lot of this has to do with the fact that it's just the natural law of growing up but maybe I went too far …

I spent a lot of time with my nieces making arts and crafts. I remember one October I was so desperate to be busy and distract myself, I sat with Lola and Eva sewing Christmas stockings, making Christmas cake and creating Christmas decorations. Even they thought it was a little early for these festivities but they happily went along with the sticking and glittering. I was already turning into the mother I was so desperate to be. The house was warm and clean and ready, I had the apron on and the cake in the oven … but the nest was still empty.

That wasn't going to be the case. That wasn't going to be my life.

I picked up the phone and I called Dr Taranissi.

*

Five Things I Was Told Would Increase My Chances of Conception

1. *Eat pineapple.*

   Pineapple contains bromelain, which is said to aid conception and help with implantation. The pineapple core is the most concentrated source of the enzyme. Bromelain can reduce inflammation in the uterus, helping to make it more receptive to a fertilised egg. An egg lives for only 12–24 hours, but sperm can live up to five days in a woman's body. So consume one section of the core five days prior to ovulation and on the day of ovulation. The pineapple should be eaten on an empty stomach for its anti-inflammatory properties. It must be fresh and raw, not canned or cooked.

2. *Lie with your legs up a wall to help the sperm get to where they need to go.*

   This is not true. Apparently data suggests that lying flat for 15 minutes may increase your chances of conception but you definitely don't have to lie with your legs up.

3. *Swim to a special rock in the sea.*

   Dayang Bunting is an island in Langkawi, off the coast of Malaysia, where Chris and I went on honeymoon. It's translated as 'Island of the Pregnant Maiden'. The legend says that a man named Mat Teja met and fell in love with the princess Mambang Sari at the freshwater lake in the middle of the island. They married and the princess soon gave birth to a son. However, their son did not live long and the grief-stricken parents decided to lay their son's body to rest in the waters of the lake. The princess blessed all women having difficulty in conceiving a child, declaring that they would become fertile if they swam in the waters. This belief endures with the locals to this day, aided by the fact that the hills that form the backdrop of the lake resemble a woman lying on her back with her belly bulging out like a pregnant woman's. I swam in this lake on my honeymoon, praying all the time I was in the water.

4. *Stop using bleach.*

   Apparently lots of chemicals can get into your skin and reduce your chances of conception. I changed all my cleaning products to Ecover and wore rubber gloves while washing up. To no avail.

5. *Laugh.*

   It is said that stress plays a huge part in not getting pregnant. I was told at this time that laughter helps the embryos to implant. Happy mother equals happy womb, so I watched *Friends* on repeat in the hope of getting up the duff.

Chapter 5

How the hell had I ended up here? This was my last resort, wasn't it? This wasn't meant to happen to me. I wasn't meant to be one of those crazy IVF women I'd read about and, more importantly, I wasn't going to be. This was going to work first time for me.

I think I genuinely felt some relief at the start of the IVF process; at least it was now being taken out of my hands and someone else could take control for a bit. It was almost like heaving a big sigh of relief that soon this journey would be over. I also thought that I would do IVF, get pregnant and then afterwards my body would be kick-started by all the hormones so I would be able to naturally conceive next time round with baby number two. That was of course if I didn't have twins! I think it's also important to say here that, even at the age of 47, there's a part of me that still hasn't given up all hope of conceiving naturally, even though that sounds insane. I think that once you have spent every single month praying it will happen, it is so hard to just switch that off. I am not sure you ever do.

I had decided that the next logical step was to go for IVF. I say 'I' here because this whole journey was being engineered by me. Chris was happy to go along with whatever I thought best. I think he just wanted his happy wife back again and if this was a way to get her, then so be it. I'm amazed that he never once complained, maybe for fear of getting his head bitten off by his highly volatile wife.

As I mentioned in the last chapter, Zita West had recommended the ARGC clinic and Dr Taranissi to me. She sent me lots of information about the clinic and the success rates and I have to say, after reading it, I defy anyone under the age of 35 to think that they didn't have a truly fighting chance of conception there. Some of the statistics were so high that, in a round of ten people, there was a 90 per cent success rate.

I cheerily read out these statistics to my husband. 'This is obviously the place to go,' I said. 'Yes it's expensive, but when you read this you can absolutely understand why. They monitor you all the way along, it's not like the NHS.' A few weeks before, we had been for a consultation at our local hospital that offered one free round of IVF on the NHS. I know things have radically changed now, but at the time there was a very low success rate and that was because they only had certain days for egg harvesting and embryo transfer, regardless of where you were in your cycle.

I had many conversations with Chris about whether we should actually go for it, even though it was very much already decided in my mind. I knew that we had a much better chance of it working if we went private and I had just enough savings from the acting jobs I had done. I had read it was about £3,000–5,000 a go, so I definitely didn't have all of it, but I had saved enough to pay most of it myself.

All my friends and family were positive about the idea. I spoke to a friend whose IVF had been successful and she had ended up with twins. My girlfriends were supportive and thought it sounded like the obvious next step. My sister put me in touch with friends of hers who had done (successful) IVF and everyone agreed that I had a definite chance of it working for me, given my age and medical history. Most people I spoke to had got pregnant within three rounds. When I read up further, that lucky number kept being bandied around and, although I had read a few horror stories of people going seven rounds, it seemed this wasn't the norm. I honestly felt that saying we would give it three goes was just to be on the safe side. I never dreamed I wouldn't get pregnant within that timespan. Chris also read all the positive articles I gave him on IVF and, as he said, he physically didn't have to do very much at all. As far as he was concerned, as long as I was OK with all the procedures that would be coming my way, he thought it was our best hope.

We went to meet Dr Taranissi on a rainy Wednesday afternoon. I rang the buzzer of the big mansion block just off Harley Street and opened the door to a hive of activity. We walked through the corridor and found the office where a lovely lady called Julie gave us some forms to fill out and told us to wait in the room next door. We found a couple of chairs and looked around. It was full of mostly women, a few men. Everyone was pretty quiet and keeping themselves to themselves. I looked up and met a woman's eye, and she gave me a look as if to say: 'Here we are, all in the same boat.' It's a funny room, an IVF waiting room, and exactly the correct term: 'waiting'. A room full of desperate hope, of anticipation, waiting for the news we all wanted to hear, waiting for our longed-for pregnancies to happen.

After a few minutes we got called upstairs to Dr Taranissi's office. I sat across from him and told him my story up until that moment of sitting in his chair. I remember being very emotional as I relayed the trauma of my ectopic and the journey that had led me to him. By this time it had been 18 months of trying and I was desperate. He listened and smiled and then sat back in his chair. 'Lisa,' he said, 'we will need to do some blood tests to check everything out, but from what you are saying, there is no reason why you can't get pregnant. I think we should start with a round of IUI before we do the IVF. It doesn't always work, but you get a good idea of the procedures and we can put the sperm into you at the optimum time.'

I had heard of IUI before – Zita had mentioned it to me. It stands for interuterine insemination. Basically, they wash the sperm and put it in a tube into your uterus at the right time in your cycle; to find this they scan you throughout your cycle to see when you are fertile and which follicle you will ovulate from.

I remember feeling like I could finally exhale and that maybe somebody had my back. It all sounded so grown up and there was so much medical jargon that I felt a little bamboozled but, ultimately, I felt like we were in safe hands. I had done a bit of research about different clinics and one thing a lot of people had said about ARGC was that, although it had the best IVF statistics in the country, it was very fast-paced and not very personal. I have to say that I didn't find this the case at all. There was always someone to talk to when I phoned up.

That said, I was quite happy to feel anonymous at the beginning of this process. It wasn't that I felt any sense of shame at what I was doing, I was just conscious that it was quite a long and invasive process where I would probably/hopefully end up putting on weight and getting pregnant. Being on TV, I didn't want anyone to know until we were out of the danger zone and ready to share our news. I suppose, if I dig a little deeper, I felt a little bit of a failure at my lack of ability to naturally conceive and, to be honest, I didn't want to have to give any press interviews about it and I didn't want everybody knowing my business. Not that I was super famous or super interesting to anyone, but it was hard enough just keeping it between some family and close friends. I think you would call it damage limitation.

As it transpired, the IUI didn't work and, looking back, I wonder how successful IUI actually is overall. I know that it can increase your chances of getting pregnant by between 10 and 20 per cent if you're aged between 20 and 35, but it definitely didn't work with anyone I knew or know now. I think it is a great way of a doctor getting to know how your body works, and what the issues are. After all, if you just need a little helping hand with fundamentally healthy organs in full working order, then there is no reason why it wouldn't have good results. Maybe by the time most people get to IVF clinics, they know their chances of conception are pretty low and IUI is a sort of safety bridge between natural conception and the huge commitment of IVF. It certainly felt like that to me. I think my age and desperation were taken into account, but Dr Taranissi had said that we would only try IUI once before going the whole hog.

It all happened so quickly. I had scans and I was initially very excited that we were trying something else at a professional clinic, where I was being properly monitored. I felt that I was in safe hands, and I must have believed this process had a good chance of working, otherwise I wouldn't have gone for it. But, in all honesty, I pretty much knew it hadn't worked the moment we did it. I don't know why – perhaps because Dr T said we should only try it the once. A couple of weeks later I remember feeling my period coming and knowing that I wasn't pregnant before I even did the test. Literally half an hour afterwards my period started. Yet again I felt like a failure; that great wave of sadness and a slight sense of impending doom started creeping in, as I began to think that maybe this wasn't going to go as smoothly as I first thought. However, I tried to look on the bright side – after all, this time I had a back-up plan in place.

It seemed everywhere I looked, people were pregnant and happy and I was a mess. I could only see one thing and that was a baby. I thought that IVF was going to solve all my troubles. On the one hand I was ready for it and excited; on the other there was that familiar background sense of dread. It felt like constant butterflies in my stomach, and in my head that feeling signifies either something exciting or something scary. Definitely something big – and IVF is a big deal, let's not try to pretend otherwise. But I was ready for it.

I remember feeling that I had to be healthy and calm and all the things I had read in the few books that were around at the time. I tried to eat well and sleep more and not to stress myself out too much but, in reality, I was so wound up. So much nervous excitement was constantly coursing through my body that I don't think I was ever really calm.

The great thing about embarking on IVF was that I had a plan. That there was stuff to do and my diary became filled with appointments for scans and blood tests, etc. It felt almost like the beginning of our pregnancy and I embraced the drug taking and tests wholeheartedly. It felt like I was finally able to take back a bit of control. I had a reason for being again; I was relevant. I had to turn up for scans and take drugs at the right times and constantly check in with the nurses at the clinic. It was exciting, and I could feel the adrenaline coursing through my veins. I was smiling again.

The clinic is a very different place depending on where you are in your cycle. I remember going in first thing in the morning and it was like a conveyor belt of women queuing for drugs and sitting waiting for scans. Some with that hopeful look on their faces. Others really angry that there were no free seats, looking completely frazzled. I got to know a few people who were at the same point in their drugs and cycle and we became 'sort of' friends.

I started my first round of IVF in the autumn of 2005. What is strange or odd or just the stars aligning is the fact that, if I had fallen pregnant then, that baby would have been born at exactly the same time as Billie. Coincidence or constellation? Was it already written in the stars?

First thing I had to have done was a hysteroscopy, to check that everything was all right with my uterus and they knew exactly what size it was and exactly where to put the embryos in. It was a very minor operation but it all went well. Next I had my blood tests done to check my hormone levels and I was then given a nasal spray to basically suppress all my natural hormones and shut down any production of follicle-stimulating hormones. I had to take it for ten days. It felt so odd that a small nasal spray had so much control over my body – funny how these small things change so much in you, but they do.

Just as the Clomid changed my moods, so did these drugs, but it was ten times worse. What they don't tell you is that you're almost sent into a menopausal state, so your emotions are all over the place. However, I had a clear goal so I took it all in my stride, or at least at the time I thought I did. Yes, I had a few headaches and I felt really ratty but it was OK, we were moving towards our goal.

Once all the hormones were inactive, I then had to start giving myself injections to stimulate my eggs. It sounds so weird and matter of fact as I write this and at the time I wasn't at all scared, just excited. The nurses were called Ellie and Julie and they were lovely and showed me how to inject myself. I had to do it at the same time every day and have regular scans to check that everything was progressing properly so that we would know the optimum time to take my eggs out.

I have had to do a lot of deep soul searching for this chapter as, for some reason, I have completely blocked out my IVF rounds from my memory – and for someone who wrote a diary for many years, it astounds me that I never documented this journey. Maybe because it was too raw. What I do remember is where I injected myself, as every time I talk about the IVF and the injections, I automatically grab the right side of my stomach. Obviously my favoured injecting spot. It's subconscious but that muscle memory is still there.

At the clinic I had been given a brown bag of medication along with my lesson on injections and had been sent home full of hope. After about 12 days my eggs were a good size and ready to be harvested. At this point you are given a 'trigger' injection that you administer at night and the eggs are collected within 36 hours of that time. That first evening I did that trigger injection, I had butterflies in my stomach and I could hardly sleep. This was the beginning of the end. The day had passed in a whirlwind of scans and blood tests and I had almost danced out of the clinic, bursting with anticipation.

That night I dreamed of babies and eggs and Dr Taranissi presenting me with my child.

I had to arrive at the clinic 36 hours after that injection. I was taken into a small changing room and given a gown to put on, then I was taken into an 'operating' room where the anaesthetist checked my ID and put a canula in my arm. I woke up a little later in a large light room with beds on either side of me, separated by screens. There were a few other women in there coming round from the same operation. I felt drowsy and woozy and I was offered a cup of tea and a digestive biscuit and, I swear, it was one of the best cups of tea and biscuits I have ever had. I think it must have been something to do with the comfort of it all. I remember feeling really taken care of.

Once the nurse had brought me the tea she told me how it had gone. I had produced eight eggs, all of which looked very good. Now all that had to be done was the eggs needed to be injected with the sperm sample Chris had given and away we would be. I was told to sit for a little while and then to get dressed and go home and relax for the rest of the day. I was a bit bleary-eyed and bloated from the procedure and couldn't wait to be on my sofa at home.

I also remember that I had to keep drinking the milk and water. From the time of the first round of injections they had advised me to drink at least a pint to a litre of full-fat milk and two litres of water every day. I was told this was to prevent hyperstimulation of my eggs and to help with the bloating. I have no idea of the science behind this and frankly

I didn't need to, I was just happy to follow instructions and do anything I could. That said, I have never been a fan of milk and to drink that quantity of the stuff filled me with horror. I would make a pint of hot chocolate and guzzle it as quickly as I could then go and clean my teeth. I couldn't stand that creamy aftertaste, but if it was going to give me all the protein I needed and keep me healthy enough to have a baby then I would do it.

After I came home from the clinic, the waiting game began. I sat on my sofa watching rubbish telly and eating nice things and genuinely feeling that I was on my road to motherhood. The clinic would call us the next morning and tell us how the eggs were doing and how many had fertilised. We were told they would call before 11 a.m. every day for the next few days, so on the first morning we were both ready by the phone, notebook in hand, to write down our scores.

It was a great start. Out of eight eggs they had injected, five had fertilised. So far so good. I remember calling my sister and telling her the news, feeling already as if I was talking about my growing baby.

The clinic called every day for three days. All was going well; the cells were doing exactly what they should be doing. They decided that they would put the embryos back in on day five. They were at the stage just before blastocyst, which is the point prior to implantation of the embryo in the uterus. The day of the transfer I had three good embryos, and Dr T put in the two healthiest and most positive looking.

I remember not wanting to get up from the bed afterwards. My husband had held my hand the whole way through and, although it was a procedure and there were other people in the room, it felt almost sacred, like this was the moment of conception. This was our moment.

Now all I had to do was go home and relax and wait ten days for the pregnancy test. I had different injections to take with me – big progesterone ones that had to be done in my bottom. I took it all in my stride. It was going to be fun. This was the beginning of our pregnancy.

While this first round of IVF was happening to me, I was also trying to live a normal life. I was auditioning for jobs and doing voiceovers and trying to act as if nothing was going on. I remember getting a recall for a great character in a new series and, just before I went in to read, I was in the loo injecting myself. A few days later I heard that I had got the job. I was due to start filming the day after the embryo transfer – in Manchester. I had to say yes to the job as the IVF was an expensive process and also I was an actress and this defined me. What if the IVF didn't work and I was left with no job and no baby? I had to take it. I asked the clinic if I would be all right to walk around and work the next day and they told me that as long as I took it easy I should be fine.

I remember coming home from the transfer and just sitting on the sofa with my legs up. I had my bags packed and had organised a driver (another huge expense) to take me up to Manchester so that I could lie on the back seat the whole way there. I arrived at my new lodgings and my best friend Ange, who was also filming up there, came to see me. She made my bed, hung fairy lights in the apartment, put throws over the sofa and made it as homely and cosy as possible. By this point she was a mother herself and had left her baby at home with her husband while she went back to work. I sat with her all evening, trying to convince both myself and her that it would all be OK. I was feeling bloated and full of milk and completely stressed from the thought of a new job, learning lines and trying to keep a lid on all of it and relax for the embryos. The only person that knew I was going through this on my new job was the producer, who was a good friend. But it was bloody hard trying to be all things to all people and proving that I was perfectly capable of doing my job while packed full of pregnancy hormones and injecting myself in the loos at work every morning.

Ten days went by without any obvious problems. I felt happy that I was working and luckily spent a lot of time on set sitting down. I had made a couple of friends in my IVF round who were going through the same thing, and we would call or text and just offer each other words of support, all waiting for our day of reckoning.

The day before my test I was at home and trying to be calm. My body felt weird, and fat. I had gone up a dress size and had a bum and boobs that I have to admit I quite liked. But I had a strange pain, like period pain. I tried to block it out, to reassure myself that it was all OK and that pregnancy pains could feel the same as period pains, but I think I knew then. I didn't feel pregnant.

I did the test, in the loo on my own. It was negative. Chris was waiting outside the door. He looked at my face and the pointless test in my hands. I just crumpled into him. He tried to make me feel better, to remind me that it was just our first go, that we could try again, that it was almost an experiment the first time. In my head I just thought it was all my fault. What if I hadn't taken the job? What if I had just stayed at home on the sofa? Would it have made a difference? Had I managed to relax enough? If I had been more chilled out, would I have been sitting here with two blue lines on my test? I think the worst thing of all was the amount of pregnancy hormones that were raging through my body. I was so emotional and bloated and full of milk. My mind was in a constant spiral of self-recrimination. My body had betrayed me again. I hadn't taken enough care of myself. I hadn't looked after that precious embryo well enough. How stupid I had been to take on a new job the day after transfer. Now I would have to wait at least three months before I could try again. I only had myself to blame.

No matter how much anyone told me that it wasn't my fault that the first round didn't work, I didn't believe them. I wallowed for ages. Now every pregnant woman I saw in the street became my nemesis. Out of the ten people to do the same round of IVF as me, only two of us didn't get pregnant. As I said earlier, I sort of made a few friends along the way, sitting in that waiting room together, but when I got the 'we are pregnant but it's very early days' texts I couldn't even feel happy for them. The other lady who didn't get pregnant already had a daughter and I remember thinking, 'Well, you're all right, you've already had a baby. You know what it's like and you're just being greedy.' As I said, those hormones really mess you up. I was never one of those people to think mean things and now all I did was scowl at people and cease communication with the successful IVFers.

Life went on. Chris and I were still trying to have sex as many times as possible in the hope that the IVF drugs would have triggered something and maybe we would conceive naturally, but to no avail. We went through a very depressing Christmas and then I started filming the second series of the show so it was six months before we tried again. In the meantime I had discovered a lovely acupuncturist called Barbara Moss. She would treat me at her home at all the right points in my cycle and gave me Chinese herbs to boost my fertility. I went to her for years, during and after the IVF. I found that, although I didn't like the needles being stuck in me, they did a great job in calming me. It was probably one of the only times that I properly rested.

Failing the first time was a massive blow, but it was like a bad Friday night at the beginning of the weekend. It wasn't great but we still had Saturday and Sunday to make it better. I also remember thinking that the first time would really have been a trial run and I convinced myself it would almost have been a fluke had we managed to get pregnant on the first go. Now Dr Taranissi knew my body and my womb and how I'd responded to the drugs, so attempt number two was going to be the one!

I psyched myself up to be in a good and positive place, so when we started round two it was pretty similar to the first. The nasal spray, the injections, the blessed milk, the blood tests. However, this time I had to do a new blood test that had recently been trialled to check my natural killer cells (the cells that kill off any foreign cells in your body as part of your body's immune system). My levels were very high. They put me on a drip of IVIG (intravenous immunoglobulin) a few days before egg collection to help suppress them. They were doing everything they could. I was also on Viagra, which gave me headaches the first few days, but it had been proven to increase the thickness of the womb lining and also help with implantation issues and improve blood supply to the right place.

This time round I sat quietly in the waiting room whenever I was at the clinic. I didn't want to talk to anyone and I realised why people in that room mostly kept themselves to themselves after their initial cycle. The hurt was too much to share and you were in a weird competition with the others. I am so glad social media was only just born as I don't think I could have stood sharing my day-to-day news on a Whatsapp group.

On the morning of my egg collection I remember actually looking forward to the tea and biscuit and the news of my eggs. This time they got six. They all looked good but the phone call the next morning was not so promising. They managed to inject three of the eggs but only one fertilised. It wasn't the best embryo and they decided to put it back in on day three. I already felt like I had failed at this point. I hadn't even managed to make it to day five! This time I had 12 days to wait until the pregnancy test, though I didn't need to wait that long as, by day ten, my period had started.

I had stayed sitting down pretty much every day after the transfer. I hadn't done anything to stress myself out. I had been calm (well, as calm as I could be). I hadn't drunk wine or caffeine. I'd lived like a nun. And nothing. No. Thing.

It was a bleak time. My sister was very happy to listen to me, but she felt so very helpless and I think I probably pushed her, and my best friends with babies, away. I would go round to my sister's and just sit at her kitchen table, moping and crying and sounding like a broken record. I would hold her babies tight and she would let me play with them, bath them and read them stories and put them to bed in the hope that it would help fill that hole a little. At the time my nieces were my only comfort. No matter how hard my friends or family listened, or how very much they supported me, they had what I wanted and I never truly felt that they understood. I know that my dad felt helpless too, and had taken to waiting for me to bring up the subject before he did, scared that he would say something wrong and get his head bitten off.

It was a very lonely experience. The only person with me in this was Chris and he wasn't actually having to go through the physical upheaval of it. He felt my pain and he very much wanted a child but, rightly or wrongly, ultimately the only person going through all of this was me.

Chris and I planned a few days away together after we got the news. We took the chance to get out of London and went for walks on the beach to blow the cobwebs away. Gradually, I felt a little better, a little stronger.

Picking myself up after another failed cycle was pretty difficult. I hear of women that have tried several times over. I take my hat off to them. Getting up off that floor and dusting yourself down ready to start again is bloody hard. As I have said before, I can't imagine what I was like to live with at this time, pumped to the hilt with hormones as I was. Crying at literally anything, angry at the world and so desperate to just get on with the next go. I turned down auditions for brilliant jobs that I just didn't have the confidence to do; I desperately needed some work as the money was running out and I wanted to do another round, but I just couldn't get up off the sofa.

Eventually I started to feel a little brighter. I still had one more go left. We went away for a few days to try to mend my broken heart. I made dinners and baked cakes in a bid to take my mind off the craziness that was going on in my head. And after a summer off I was ready to start again. I had been told by Dr T that there was no definitive reason why I couldn't conceive and each time we tried he adjusted the drugs and procedures accordingly, to give us the optimum chance.

My third and final go. This had to be the one. It was autumn: the leaves were turning, the sun was shining and, although it was low in the sky, I could feel hope in the air. Maybe, just maybe, this Christmas I would be pregnant.

Again everything seemed to go to plan. My eggs were collected. Six, just like the last time. They injected five and decided to put three back in on day three. The embryos looked good and Dr Taranissi knew that it was my last chance. I had said upfront that we only had enough money for three tries and Dr T had said that after three rounds he would have done everything possible to make me conceive. I know some women go on to have many more tries, but it's usually at different clinics or because something fixable went wrong in previous rounds, so maybe there were other options for them. I knew that wasn't the case for me.

In terms of appearance, everything looked textbook but, as Dr T said, the embryos are only half the story. Your body has to be ready to be a mother. It has to welcome those little foreign cells and implant them – and I was ready. I was eating healthily, sleeping well, drinking pints and pints of milk and keeping very much to my side of the bargain. Those embryos just needed to keep to theirs.

This time, when we went home again I did very little. I had heard from someone that laughter was really good for your body while waiting for the embryos to implant so I ordered the *Friends* box set of videos and watched them all on a loop, feeling fat and happy. However, the fact that Dr T had put three embryos in kept niggling at me. Why had he done that? Obviously he'd thought one of them wasn't very good. He hadn't said that at all, in fact he said all three were doing exactly what they should have been doing at the time of transfer, but being the worrier that I have always been, I didn't quite buy it. Was it last chance saloon time and I had just looked so desperate? Stop thinking, Lisa!

After 12 days of waiting, driving myself slowly mad, I did the pregnancy test. We had bought a few. All hopes depended on this and I did feel slightly different. There could be a chance, couldn't there?

I did the test. It was negative. One blue line, never two. This was my last go, my final chance and it hadn't worked. I was distraught. I phoned ARGC and they told me to come in and see Dr Taranissi. Chris and I were both so sad and done in but we dutifully made our way to Wimpole Street. I hated going back into that clinic, seeing the bright faces, the busy women on their busy IVF treadmill, picking up their brown paper bags of hope. We sat in a corner until we were called upstairs. I tried to be brave, to give Dr T a smile but it just turned into a blub and before I knew it I was completely undone. Again.

He sat me down. 'Lisa,' he said, 'I can do all the things, I can check and monitor you, I can change your doses and make sure that all your embryos look good when I put them back, but I can't do the magic. And for that reason I am going to let you go.'

The magic, the bloody magic! Why couldn't he do that? He could get so many people pregnant and yet here I was, a healthy, young(ish) woman with the world at her feet and he was advising me to stop. What could he see that I couldn't? Many women go on to have many more IVF attempts, why wasn't he begging me to try just one more round?

I couldn't really see anything clearly at the time. I know that Chris was next to me and obviously acutely aware that I was at the end of my tether with it, and we were both in a bit of a daze. I think the word I'm looking for is shock.

I nodded like one of those dogs on the back seat of cars. I made all the right noises and said I understood but inside I just felt numb. He was letting me go. My body couldn't do the magic. He had done everything he could for me. I looked back at the past 18 months. The lows and dark days of the ectopic, the Clomid, the fertility sticks, the highs of the IVF, the madness of the drugs and injections that had all become so normal … and I felt lost. Small and lost and sad. Emotionally drained, physically exhausted. Completely broke. I was done.

Fourteen years on and in the process of writing this book I realise I have a complete mental block about my IVF journey. For some reason I have shut it all out of my mind. I remember injecting myself, I remember getting fat and bloated but not much else. I decided to call the ARGC.

Dr Taranissi apparently remembers me very well, and as the lady on the phone tells me this, I feel a great gulp in my throat, a long-buried sadness as yet again I'm reduced to tears at what never was, what I never could do.

What would have happened had it worked out? How would I feel? Who would I be? Why does it hurt so very much? Still?

I suppose there's a hole inside me that has never been filled. Just as there is a hole in my daughter, a grief that she holds, which will never be filled. We are united in that. We have and will continue to help each other mend, and slowly and hopefully those holes will be filled. It's obviously an ongoing process, like all grief is.

Dr Taranissi agrees to meet me to talk me through my treatment. I don't know if this will help me, or help this book in any way. I don't know if it will go some way to holding someone else's hand as they embark upon their own roller coaster. I hope so.

I meet up with Dr Taranissi on a sunny Wednesday afternoon. Just walking into the clinic my memories come flooding back. It hasn't changed at all. The waiting room is still the same, the photos of grinning babies adorning the walls. I give him a hug and yet again my eyes start watering. I tell him how very important he was in my life, that although IVF hadn't worked for me, years later I see it as only a positive experience. I would still advise anyone to do it, and am happy to recommend this brilliant, kind and caring man, who never stops working and sees everybody as an individual.

I have one question for him. Why did he let me go? I have always just simply stated to people word for word what he had said to me, and for whatever reason, friends and family have never pressed it. I suppose it made absolute sense to them but years later it was still niggling at me. Women do IVF many, many times but after three attempts he told me it was enough, and he'd said the line about the magic. Why?

Dr T tells me that he had tried everything he could at that time. He had monitored me so closely and I was clearly emotionally done with the process. He could see it in my eyes. I was fragile. When he reminds me of my state, I almost feel like he is talking about someone else. In my mind I had put such a game face on, ready to keep going and keep going, whatever cost. But to the outside world, and more especially to him, it was glaringly obvious that I wasn't emotionally strong enough to go through a process that could very well end up in failure again. He says that most women have three rounds of IVF when they go there; they may have had plenty of tries elsewhere but usually by the time they get to ARGC it's their last hope. He says his high success rate is still the same, and usually if it's going to succeed it will do so within those three cycles. He tells me that he was absolutely sure that my problem was an implantation issue. There has been a lot more research now and, although it's still the hardest thing to 'cure', there are a few other things available to try nowadays.

We talk a lot. I tell him that I am very honoured that he remembers me. I show him a picture of my daughter and tell him what she had said to me that morning.

'Mama, aren't you pleased that the IVF didn't work because if it had you wouldn't have had me?'

I replied, 'Actually, Billie, I am.' And I meant it with all my heart. That hole is getting smaller.

There are big chunks of sunlight ahead. I promise you.

While in the middle of the IVF process, when the embryos were put back snugly inside me, I really wanted to look after myself. I didn't want to take any drugs or painkillers that

I didn't need to and which might harm my 'babies'. I remember getting quite a few colds and making up the best all-natural and non-harmful cold cure. It has got me through many a cold winter since.

Natural Cold Cure

You will need:
1 'finger' of fresh turmeric, peeled
1 inch fresh ginger, peeled
2 tsp manuka honey
juice of half a lemon
hot water

Method:
Chop the turmeric and ginger finely and put in a mug with the honey and lemon. Top with hot water. Leave to infuse for 5 minutes then drink.

Chapter 6

For many people, their quest for a baby finishes in Chapter Five. They go through IVF and, after a series of failed cycles, they are done. Believe me, I know what it is like to feel done. I found my three attempts extremely emotionally and physically draining. I know that lots of women go on to have many more than three cycles (and to some, three doesn't seem like a huge amount) and I take my hat off to them.

It was such a complicated time: a small part of me was relieved that, physically, I didn't have to put my body through that again. No more injections or tablets or blood tests. It was yet another avenue I had exhausted, another path that had led to a miserable dead end, and the worst of it was that I had seen IVF as the Holy Grail; I had seen myself as a definite and I was now a definitely not. I think I was too mentally exhausted to really process it and, instead, I let the relief at no longer having to be a human pin cushion wash over me.

But the other part of me couldn't help but wonder if we should keep going. The problem is that it is so easy to get addicted to hope; it is part of the human condition. Fertility treatment is the ultimate in Russian roulette. Every roll of the dice offers new odds and a chance to finally succeed at the one thing most people find easy. With all its highs and lows that sense of addiction creeps in fast. In the same way as an addict needs just one more drink, or hit, or hand of cards, there is always the chance of one more go to get what you want, believing that this time the odds will almost certainly be in your favour. I just couldn't process that I was 33 years old and completely infertile. People find money from nowhere, practically bankrupting themselves, for their one more chance. I was no different; I had no more money left, though I'm sure I would have found some if the option was open to me. But I had one major thing halting me and that was Dr Taranissi.

In a way I feel lucky that Dr Taranissi actually curbed the misery of my expectation by putting an end to my attempts. He could see I was emotionally drained from the experience and that he had done all he could. As he had said, he couldn't do the magic and he'd tried all that was viable at the time. Any more goes would have just been a game of chance, and he had carefully and patiently explained that there was no more to be done for me. I think, had money been no object, I might have potentially persuaded him to let me go again, but the river was dry and, somewhere deep down in my gut, I knew that this wasn't going to be my way of becoming a mother.

It was emotional, but my IVF journey was definitely over. Even though he didn't manage to get me pregnant, Dr Taranissi is still my hero and I feel very strongly that he was the best doctor to go to. If anyone could have been successful, it would have been him. But loving your doctor doesn't help you leave the clinic feeling anything other than empty-handed. It is the ultimate consolation prize and nothing changed that. I was sad and exhausted. I had to take a breath.

So for a while, I gave myself a break, trying to put some distance between myself and the emotional roller coaster I had just ridden, trying to stop beating myself up about why it hadn't worked out for me. But, once I'd taken stock, I knew I couldn't give it up. I realised that whatever I chose to do next would take me firmly off my biological path of having a baby and I had to come to terms with that. I had got further and further away from my original goal, quietly changing the position of the posts to suit my needs. And it was only going to get worse. The failed cycles of IVF had definitely made me more pragmatic and, somehow, I managed to dig deep and summon the strength to keep going.

I wouldn't give it up, and I wouldn't let it go. It felt like I was wired and ready to try the next possibility. Despite all the disappointment that kept coming, actually, my desire for a baby was more intense than ever. It wasn't showing any signs of fading into the background. At this point I could feel that my friends (through no fault of their own) had backed off. I had dug myself into a little hole of loneliness and self-absorption. Nobody knew what to say to me or what I could do next. Had they given me any advice, I wouldn't have listened to it. I was certain that only I knew best. The only person that could talk to me was Chris, and even he knew it was fruitless arguing or trying to stop me from searching for the next thing. The next fix that would solve my problem and mend my broken heart. He kept quiet and let me spin; after all, we both wanted a baby so desperately. I know I felt lonely at this time, but I had let go of all normality really. I needed help and conventional medicine had failed me.

So, I couldn't grow my own baby, but I still ached for one. I wracked my brains for what to do next. Could someone else grow it for me? I remembered hearing about the surrogate Kim Cotton and I knew she had set up a charity called COTS. I'd seen an interview with her on *This Morning* and I must have filed it away in my brain under the section of 'impossibilities and last resorts'. My mind very happily retrieved this information and my inner self was extremely pleased with my resourcefulness: 'See, you knew it would come in handy one day!'

Kim had been in the press a lot when I was younger. The majority of the reports were positive: she had been the UK's first surrogate mother, and she had given the gift of a baby to a couple who had lost all hope of ever becoming parents. She had carried out a wonderfully selfless act and changed their lives forever. It was a magical story and she wanted to give other couples in similar situations the ability to realise their dreams. What a wonderful thing to do. The trouble was that, in every interview, the focus was whether the surrogate would give up the child after carrying it for nine months. The horror stories were discussed at length and each interview seemed to be tinged with the trepidation of the unknown.

Surrogacy was almost viewed in this country at the time as the suspicious new kid on the block. If you entered the world of surrogacy, you were definitely taking one foot out of the traditional baby route and creeping nearer and nearer to unchartered and uncertain territory. A world of huge risks. Already the alarm bells had started to sound, but I couldn't hear them, or I wasn't listening. This was an area that I knew very little about. It was a massive step away from IVF; I was talking or thinking about a stranger doing the most intimate thing possible – handing me the yearned-for gift of a baby – yet at the time it seemed completely logical.

I called my friends and my sister, pretending to talk it through when, in reality, I had already made up my mind to pursue it. They arrived en masse for a cup of tea and my ever-practical mate, Ange, dived in with questions on statistics:

'Have you found out how many babies were born through surrogates and how many actually were given to the parents versus those kept by the surrogate?'

'Well, no, I haven't checked that out yet. But all the articles I've read and stuff I've found on the internet seem pretty positive. You are always going to hear the bad stories, as they're the ones to make the papers, don't you think?' I asked pleadingly.

'OK,' Nicola interrupted. 'But how does the process work? Will it be your baby or the surrogate's? Is it your egg or hers?'

Again, I didn't have any clear answers. 'This is all something I'm going to look into,' I curtly replied. The conversation wasn't flowing as I wanted. In my mind, all that my friends needed to do was agree that this was the next and best course of action for me, not throw spanners in the works with all their questions. Obviously, all of their concern centred around whether or not I would actually get to keep the baby. They soon gave up the questions as I promised them I would look into it properly. They assured me that they really were on my side and that they trusted that, if I wanted to go down this path, it would be because it was the right one.

I knew they'd be there the whole way. They knew my pain; they knew that the only thing to fix it would be a child; they wanted to help and yet felt so helpless. Talking to Angela years later, she told me that she had gone home and had a conversation with her husband as to whether she could carry a baby for me. My sister Victoria and I also talked about it. I clearly recall building up the courage to test the water and see if she would be horrified. We were sitting around her kitchen table; there had been endless tears about the fact that yet another IVF round hadn't worked, and I took a deep breath and said: 'Well, maybe you could do it for me.' I let out a forced laugh, just to take the edge off the biggest favour I'd ever asked of anyone. Victoria looked at me and said she would think about it. I remember gabbling away after that, saying that it could work as she had her two wonderful girls and her perfect family was complete. She stopped me dead in my tracks when she answered: 'But I'm not sure that I'm completely done having kids yet.' It hadn't even occurred to me she would go for a third – here I was, not able to even have one! That really shook me and, knowing that my sister hadn't closed the door on more kids, I didn't ever bring up the surrogacy idea again. I think it must have been torture to have said no to me, so we let it lie, words hanging unspoken saying everything they needed to.

When I look back, though, all I can think is how lucky I am that both Ange and my sister would even consider doing such a thing for me. What a truly blessed woman I am to have people who love and care about me, to the point that they would even think about having a child for me. Something I'm not sure I could have done myself had I been the fertile one.

So, it was back to the drawing board and a stranger surrogate. I had been given the green light from my friends, and my imagination was allowed to roam free. Already my head was filling with images of me and the surrogate becoming firm friends, her coming over for dinner and me rubbing her feet and singing to her bump and being present at the birth of our child, helping her to push and encouraging her on. More images played in my brain: us christening said child and the surrogate being its godmother. Me sending photos every year and chatting to her on the phone, filling her in on how our baby was developing. So I got online and started searching, hoping against all odds that this was going to save me.

I know that my mental state wasn't healthy here. This had to be a plan that was going to work this time. I knew, and my friends knew, that I would be so devastated if this didn't work, if I was rejected again. I wouldn't even entertain the niggling worry that I may never actually become a mother. If that thought had the audacity to enter my head I would shut it down immediately, sticking my fingers in my ears and singing 'la-la-la'. There was no way I was going to contemplate life without a baby. There were those days where I sat in my dressing gown, drinking tea, watching daytime telly and feeling like I couldn't get up and go on. There was no life for me without a child in it. Some days did sometimes seem endless and pointless. But I am always an optimist; it's in my blood. The sun will always come out eventually, even if it's only enough for me to have a bath, get dressed and get online.

Surrogacy has come a long way in 13 years. I looked at the COTS website for reference the other day, and was amazed at the support network and how much the charity had grown. Now a lot of fertility clinics recognise surrogacy and work alongside the charity. There are also a lot of private agencies that can organise a surrogate for you. Then it was all very different. There was only the COTS charity and still so much remained unknown because the conversation wasn't as open as it is now.

I started my search with zero information and no real frames of reference. It felt like a secret world I had entered. I didn't really even know if surrogacy was an option, and the narrative surrounding it at that time was a bit off-putting. I had heard horror stories about surrogates keeping babies and I didn't know how the whole money process worked – it made it sound a little like you were buying a baby, but I knew it couldn't be as basic as that. The only information out there didn't make it sound like a particularly developed avenue, but I decided that I wanted to dig a bit deeper. So I got on the phone to COTS.

I spoke to a lovely man, who said that he could come and visit me at home and talk me through the whole process. That's how small the charity was at the time. He sounded so very positive and upbeat and I could feel that familiar sense of excitement bubbling up inside me again. A frenzied, feverish butterfly feeling that built every time a new possibility opened up to me and I had something else to try. That hope wasn't yet gone; that inner addict was rearing its desperate head at the possibility of one last buzz that would end all the suffering. He had arranged to come on a Sunday morning and I ran around all weekend tidying the house and buying flowers to put in vases and baking. I made a coffee walnut cake *and* some chocolate brownies. I wanted to make a really good impression! I wanted him to see me for the fantastic homemaker and mother I was waiting to be.

The doorbell rang and I showed the man into the front room. I asked if he wanted tea and cake, but he said that he was fine with instant coffee and would just get on with talking us through the process. We sat on the sofa and listened as he explained that surrogacy is a wonderful thing and that there are usually two ways it works. Either the husband gives a sperm sample, so it's his sperm and the surrogate's egg, or you can use IVF with your own egg and your husband's sperm making an embryo that is then transferred into the surrogate's womb. He said that the former was by far the easier and the less expensive option, but that IVF was getting more popular.

What we would first have to do is write a letter to the potential surrogates explaining who we were and why we so desperately wanted a child. He showed us an album, one of those old eighties ones with the sticky-back paper to protect the photos, which contained smiling photos of surrogates and happy couples holding babies and some examples of letters that we would need to write. There was definitely no gloss or glamour about it. No money had been spent on shiny brochures making the process seem picture-perfect.

As I looked through the pages, my heart sank. I could literally feel the high wearing off at an alarming rate and the fantasy film playing in my head started to fade. We would have to write a brilliant letter selling ourselves, desperately hoping a surrogate would read it and something would resonate in order for them to choose us. You don't choose a surrogate. They choose you, all on the back of a simple letter.

I felt like I had less control than ever before. At least with IVF I could take the medication and be as healthy as possible. OK, my body wouldn't do what I wanted it to, but the reality was that every process I had tried thus far had been on my terms. I had decided to put my body through it; I had dictated how much I was prepared to do. Now this was another step away from the driving seat. I was firmly strapped in the back and holding on for dear life. I had no control over this. It didn't matter how much I wanted this or what I was prepared to do – I could write what I thought was the slickest, most honest, heart-wrenching letter ever and they still might not pick me.

Then there was the cost. It is illegal to pay a surrogate but you can give 'expenses' and they recommended between £12,000 and £15,000. I had no money left: the IVF had seen to that. If I wanted a baby of my own, using a womb for hire, I would have to pay for more IVF on top of the expenses. If we went down the easier route, then essentially my husband would have a baby with another woman. And then there was the letter. Reading the examples of other people's letters made my ears ring. Just the thought of writing something like that, the thought of selling ourselves to people who might not think us worthy, jumping through hoops to be the perfect couple – it was awful. What could I possibly write that hadn't been written before? What made me so special? Here I was, preparing to tell my whole sorry story to a stranger for the umpteenth time and begging to be chosen. I felt sick at having to write it. Exhausted without even having put pen to paper. I was drained of emotion and too proud to beg.

I wasn't sure I could handle the rejection. In fact, I knew I couldn't handle it.

As I said before, surrogacy is now a much more acknowledged and acceptable option and lots of people are doing it but, back then, there was something about it that just didn't sit right with me. I think it was the fact that there was no absolute guarantee that the surrogate would give us the baby. Was I just exposing myself to charlatans, who would grab my money and run? I did that research my friends begged me to do and realised that I would have no legal rights over the child – I could essentially end up with nothing and in huge amounts of debt. The thought of going through all that after the IVF and then something going wrong … it would have sent me right over the edge, and believe me I wasn't far from it. I couldn't handle any more disappointment, any more uncertainties.

I also kept thinking about my husband making a baby with a stranger. Her egg and his sperm. Would he undermine my parenting, because the baby wasn't mine but was half his? Would he become the primary carer because of this? I certainly didn't want that. I wanted to be the mother. But a stranger would always be the child's birth mother. She would forever more have a seat at my table. Was I actually ready for that? Was I sure I could handle it? I would have to think longer and even harder about this in the months to come, when adoption became my only option. But here and now, I was unconsciously setting myself up for it. Mulling over the hardest questions in the darkest depths of my mind, digging deeper than I ever thought possible.

Then there was the other option, of course – we could go down the IVF route. But just the thought of that made me want to cry. Even if we had the money, the idea of having to go through IVF again, the injections and drugs to get my eggs perfect, the implantation process and then the agonising wait for the phone call to say that the surrogate was pregnant – it was all hideous. Knowing that if it didn't work we would have to go through all that heartache again at such a huge cost. No, I definitely didn't think I could go there.

So then, how did I really feel about my husband having another woman's baby? I'd like to tell you that Chris and I sat up late into the night for days discussing what it would mean for him to, essentially, have a child with someone else. I'd like to say that we made endless careful lists of all the pros and cons, but we didn't. Of course, we talked about it. He said that if it was what I wanted he didn't see a problem with it; after all, it would be done with a sperm sample, he wouldn't actually have to have sex with a stranger. I'd like to say that I properly thought about his answer and saw the madwoman I had become, but I didn't. The baby trail is an addiction: when you're in it you're unaware that you're an addict and, to some extent, that was what I was. This was a huge life-changing moment, a massive big deal – my partner and a stranger having a child – and here I was, taking it all in my stride and being absolutely fine with it.

It is worth me saying here that I completely understand why this would be an option for some people, and I really don't have a problem with that. I'm not judging anyone in the quest to find your family. It's just that I didn't give myself the time to even look at the option logically. I didn't have the brain capacity to see anything clearly and make any sort of informed decision. My eyes were so firmly glued on the prize that it took up my whole field of vision.

I was the one driving everything and here I was, contemplating an avenue that physically excluded me from every part of the process. How would I really feel about my husband making a baby with a stranger and then me merrily taking it on as my own, his eyes and an unknown nose staring back at me? It would be like handing someone the keys to my life.

I couldn't shake off the image of a desperate, barren woman next to a fertile goddess and that was absolutely no good for my ever-diminishing self-esteem. Highlighting my feeble body and my flaws wouldn't help my fragile state. I would be a first-time mother grappling with a birth mother who may know how to deal with it all much better than me. Would I be on the phone to her, asking advice on how to get the baby (her baby) off to sleep? Would she be the one I'd call to ask medical questions that I didn't know the answers to? Did I want this constant reminder of my body's failure in my life? Little did I know that many of the issues that ultimately led me to knock back this option were the same issues I would be facing in the future when I decided to adopt.

But I wasn't there yet and so I thanked the kind man with the big bag and the photo albums and threw the uneaten cake in the bin. In a matter of hours, my hope had yet again crashed against the rocks, disappearing in front of me in a foam of watery nothingness. Exhaustion flowed through me and my shoulders slumped – I felt the smallest I had felt in a long while. The wind had been well and truly knocked out of my sails for the umpteenth time.

I think what ultimately got me about surrogacy was the uncertainty. There were no definites. I had thought about loving a child that wasn't mine, but that was half my husband's, and I could almost tick that off my list as a yes. I could possibly cope with another mother in my life for eternity. I could step aside and hold the child's other hand, so another yes was ticked. The big stumbling point, the big no, was the letter. The anger that I felt at having to write it reared up inside me like a dragon breathing fire, the pure injustice of it all. I wasn't prepared to write a letter, not because it wasn't worth it – the prize was definitely worth doing anything for – but the thought of it hurt me so much. Why did someone else get to decide if I was good enough? How could they tell on the basis of a few written words? I needed more control over my destiny. Nobody was going to make the biggest decision of my life for me. I couldn't get past it and I knew in the pit of my stomach that this wasn't going to be an option for me.

One night a few weeks later, still dazed from the aftermath, after a lot of talking and the usual tears, Chris tentatively said to me: 'Why don't we adopt?' I know he was scared to broach the subject. For weeks we had sat, defeated, on the sofa. He knew he had to do something; we couldn't just sit there staring at the television screen every night but not actually watching it any more. I had to get out of my dressing gown and out of the house. I had to open the blinds and let some air in, some light. I swallowed and opened my mouth to speak.

'I'm not sure I could.'

'Why?'

'Because it wouldn't be my child. I wouldn't have made it or grown it, and it wouldn't even be part of you. I just don't know.'

'Well, as a man, I don't grow a baby, I don't really have anything to do with it until it's born and put in my arms, and I love it from that moment on. I don't see much difference in doing that with an adopted child.'

I listened to his words.

I definitely wanted to be a mother. The route had changed but the goal was still exactly the same.

I have since spoken to my sister about this, wondering if the rest of the family were worried at yet another new obsession when I first mentioned adoption. I had this idea that they were all huddled in a corner talking about how crazy I was. But she said they were all actually really relaxed about it and were just delighted there was still hope of some description. Victoria said: 'You were so focused and convinced this was the way you would become a mother, we all got swept along with you. All I wanted was for you be a mummy, I wanted it so badly for you. It didn't really matter how it happened. Also, we all know that once you get something in your head, there's no stopping you.'

She wasn't wrong. All of a sudden, a new pathway had opened up in front of me.

I couldn't leave this chapter without the addition of the recipe for the coffee walnut cake I made to impress the COTS man. It was one of the best recipes and sadly I can't find the original. I spoke to my lovely friend Jo Wheatley and she shared hers with me, which is pretty damn good. All these years later I feel sad that I just chucked it in the bin and didn't sit with a cup of tea on the sofa and eat the whole thing.

Jo's Coffee Walnut Cake

You will need:
200g softened butter
200g caster sugar

4 large eggs, beaten

220g self-raising flour

100g finely chopped walnut pieces

25ml espresso or 1 tbsp instant coffee mixed with 25ml of boiling water, left to cool completely

Buttercream

200g butter

500g icing sugar

25ml espresso or 1 tbsp of instant coffee mixed with 25ml hot water, left to cool completely

100g walnuts pieces to decorate

You will also need two 20cm (8-inch) sandwich tins, greased and lined with a disc of buttered baking parchment.

Method:

Preheat the oven to 170°C/gas mark 4.

Beat together the butter and sugar until light and creamy. In a small bowl beat together the eggs, then slowly whisk them into the butter and sugar. Fold in the flour and walnut pieces, and finally fold in the coffee.

Divide the batter evenly between the prepared cake tins and spread level using a palette knife. Bake on the middle shelf of the preheated oven for about 25–30 minutes or until golden, well risen, and a skewer inserted into the middle of the cakes comes out clean.

Remove from the oven and carefully turn the cakes out of the tins onto wire cooling racks. Peel off the parchment and leave to cool.

To make the buttercream, whip together the butter, icing sugar and coffee until the mixture is light and fluffy.

Place one of the cooled cakes on a serving plate or cake stand right side up and spread with half the buttercream. Top with the second cake and cover with the remaining buttercream. Decorate with the walnut halves to serve.

Chapter 7

As I lay in bed I recalled a long-ago conversation in another bed with another man, years before. We were a tangle of sheets and limbs when he asked me: 'So, do you want to have kids?'

'Yes,' I answered. 'Sure. I want about five I think, at some point. Why, do you?'

'Yes, but when we have them I think we should have some of our own and some that we adopt.'

'OK,' I said quickly. I had never even considered adopting; it wasn't something I ever felt a burning desire to do.

'I've always wanted to adopt. I think it's great. There are so many children that need homes. I definitely want to do both.'

'Yeah, we can do both,' I said, cuddling into him, still basking in that first-love glow, more excited that he was obviously serious about us, and talking about us having children together, than the actual ins and outs of how many and whether we would be adopting or not. I'd said yes, but in my head I was thinking, 'Yeah, sure, he'll forget all that when we have our own, which is so far away anyway I'm not even going to entertain this yet ... yada yada yada. Let's open some more wine and stay in bed all day.'

Now, years later, here I lay, being forced to think seriously about adoption. Oh, how ignorance is bliss. You can be as cavalier as you want when you think your body is going to do what it's supposed to do, and also doubly cavalier when you don't want the end result all that much anyway. I hadn't even thought about having kids at that point, let alone adopting, and it was easy to bat it away and party on. Now I had to really dig deep and think about it. Gone was the suggestion of having my own children with a little adopted child on the side; that was all in the past, along with the ex-boyfriend. Here I was, a relatively new and infertile wife, lying in bed in the dark, contemplating my plan B.

I struggled. I lay there feeling hot under the weight of the covers and the weight on my mind. I was cross that I had to think about this seriously, cross that fate hadn't done its thing and intervened, as it had in the past when I'd needed a boyfriend or a new job. In fact, fate was nowhere to be seen. I felt horrible and I couldn't understand it. What was I kicking against? I was angry at my body and angry that I was back at square one. I didn't want to have to be different yet again. I'd already felt different when I lost my mum at such a young age, meaning I didn't do my A levels and started work before any of my friends. Despite the fact some thought I enjoyed rebellion, there was a huge part of me that was desperate to conform. My dream was to live a lovely, calm, straightforward drama-free life with 2.4 children. Instead, here I was looking terribly brave and alternative from the outside, when it was actually the only choice available based on what life had thrown at me.

What I would have given to be someone with a nice, normal job – a French teacher, say – with a mother who was alive and well, living in a suburban semi with a blooming bump. But that wasn't going to happen and there was little point in dwelling on it. My brain whirred with my husband's words about his openness towards the idea of adopting. I hadn't quite seen it the way he had. He seemed confident he could love a child that he hadn't made, that it made absolutely no difference to him whether the child was biologically his or not. Perhaps it made sense. After all, I had two beautiful nieces and godchildren and I loved all of them unconditionally without even thinking about it. Maybe I could love a child that I hadn't created?

Maybe I was that person. Maybe this could be my route to motherhood. My mind went round and round, endlessly going over the pros and cons, until the waves of sleep finally washed over me.

The next person I spoke to about the subject was my ever-supportive sister. What did she really think about my new notion, having had two babies of her own? Could I love a child that wasn't physically mine and not related to us in any way? As ever, she gave me great advice and reminded me of the Khalil Gibran quote, that children don't belong to us but are 'sons and daughters of Life's longing for itself'.

It really resonated with me. This ownership we seem to want to have over our children isn't a healthy impulse. If a child is not our blood, does that make them unworthy of our love? It suddenly hit me: I had to let go of that ownership, of that need to possess another human being made in my own image, of that desire to produce something that was mine, which I had been 'clever' enough to make. I had to grieve the fact that I would never grow a baby and put it behind me. That process was definitely well under way. In fact I was now at the point where I knew I could definitely love a baby if I hadn't made it myself. A brand-new, shiny, clean, untouched, unharmed baby ...

I started looking at adoptive mothers in the public eye. Of course, the first names that sprang to mind were Angelina Jolie and Madonna, two women I had great respect for – but could I really identify with them? They had nannies and chefs and money; they could fly their children all over the world with them. They lived a life that was so far removed from mine, I couldn't identify in any way with their path to motherhood. I'm sure if one of them decided to write a book about their experiences as an adoptive mother, I would definitely read a few things that resonated with me, but neither of them had. All I saw of their lives were carefully constructed paparazzi shots of happy, smiley rainbow families. Ever-growing broods of children with no anxiety whatsoever. I know that isn't the reality, but when that's all you're shown, how are you meant to know any different?

Any other examples of people adopting instantly made me think of very worthy 'churchy' people, who were selfless and loving and without obvious flaws. They did it just for the children, yet I was quite honest that my driving force was that I wanted to be a mother. I know these are raging stereotypes but honestly, to me at the time, that was all there was. I wasn't looking at adoption to be worthy; I just wanted to be a mum. Pure and simple.

Chris's words were constantly ringing in my ears and I was slowly getting my head around it. I had demonstrated almost daily with my sister's family how very much I loved my nieces. I had been a sponge, watching and learning from my sister how to parent.

One of the great ironies is that, having rejected surrogacy for all the reasons I have discussed, the one thing that didn't ring any alarm bells at this point was the fact that this child would always have another mother. A birth mother. Becoming a mother to a child with a mother already, how did that sit with me? How did I feel about it? In moments of clarity, it was all good, as I felt like I was a pretty generous person. I told myself that I was always happy to share, that I didn't need complete ownership over my child. I just wanted to love it, to nurture and help it along this rocky road of life. But in the dark, in the middle of the night, I wasn't entirely sure I could handle it. It would be a lot to take on. Did I have the strength and the openness of mind to be able to truly cope?

By this point, I had definitely taken myself out of the equation and left behind any thoughts or angst about a baby not being physically mine (that's not to say we weren't still trying and praying for a miracle every month). I could deal with that now. My prize was ultimately the same, just packaged differently.

I had recently seen a picture of an American actress in a gossip magazine with her brand-new adopted baby. I had torn it out and kept it with me, proof that this could happen to me. Then a few weeks later I happened upon another picture of an American pop star, again with a brand-new adopted baby. How had they managed to do it?

When I went online and scoured the internet, what became clear to me very quickly was that there wasn't any organisation that would hold my hand through this in the UK. All the examples I could see were in America. I just had to find out how they had done it over there.

I think you have probably gauged by now how very persistent I can be when I need to be, and I wracked my brains for anyone I knew who could help me.

One person immediately came to mind. I had an ex-boyfriend who was godfather to my nieces and enough time had passed for us to consider each other friends. He was living and working in LA as an actor, and he definitely knew a few of the people I had been reading about – well, he had worked with them, at least. Surely he could help me? I called him, forgetting the time difference. It was 10 a.m. for me, which meant 2 a.m. for him, and he was fast asleep when I called. But very kindly and patiently, he listened as I garbled my whole sorry story to him, how I had read about these women and did he know them and could he ask them? And if so, when? And how long would it take?

He told me he did know someone and he would contact them in the morning and call me as soon as he had any information. Bless him, and bless his girlfriend even more, who at the time was lying in bed next to him listening to the rants of a crazy ex-girlfriend!

He called later that day. Thank the Lord he did as I don't know what I would have done with myself if I'd had to wait any longer. Waiting for information was like waiting for my drugs fix or waiting for my pregnancy test. He had spoken to a friend and found the name of a solicitor who arranged these adoptions. He gave me his name and phone number and wished me all the best. I thanked him and thanked him and cried and thanked him some more.

And then I called the lawyer. I sat cross-legged on my bedroom floor, notebook in hand and the scribbled piece of paper with the number on before me. I picked up the phone and dialled the number, my heart in my mouth. Hearing the American ring tone was enough to get me giddy.

Within seconds, I was talking to the lawyer's secretary. 'Er, hello,' I said in my best Received Pronunciation actress voice, 'would it be possible to speak to the man that makes all the adoptions happen?'

'What's your name? Hold the line,' she said. I could feel the camera above my head, the camera I always picture in situations that I can't quite cope with. Here I was on the phone to the man who could possibly change my life.

'Hello, Lisa.' A strong, kind, American voice came on the line. 'How can I help you today?'

'Well, I was given your number by a friend. I know you arrange adoptions in the US, but I am in the UK, so is it possible that you could help me? I have tried and failed at IVF and we have looked into surrogacy, but I think the way forward may be adoption.'

And then I asked all the burning questions that were desperate to escape my lips. How long would the process take? How much would it cost? How easy would it actually be? It felt so surreal, the ease of getting all this information. I was almost on a high because I felt relevant again: I felt in control and there was something I could do. I was back in the driving seat of my own destiny once more. It was almost as if I were doing it for someone else, enquiring for a friend.

Yes, he could arrange an adoption for me. Yes, we would have to go over to the US at some point. But first we would have to get a home study report done with an agency in America that would put us in touch with someone in the UK.

I had no idea what a home study report was, let alone how to get one. But I soon learned that it is required for every adoption, whether it is an international or a domestic one. This study is a basic overview of your life – including a criminal background check, a report on your finances and even an examination of your personal relationships. It is often the lengthiest step when preparing to adopt and it is carried out by a social worker.

We would need to obtain a visa for the baby and would have travel costs and medical costs and expenses for the birth mother. He told me that the mothers were all HIV-, drug- and alcohol-tested and I could possibly have a baby in a matter of six months to a year. My heartbeat was quickening. So how much? And what would I have to do?

I have to say that during that conversation I couldn't work out how much in entirety it would cost, but I later figured out that a ballpark figure would be at least $50,000. I also didn't ask any questions about the mothers at the time, which, retrospectively, makes me realise the level of mania I was in. I didn't have headspace to consider anything else other than the baby.

I now know that there are agencies in the USA that help unmarried or young women, whose families can be very religious, to place their babies for adoption if they don't want to or can't keep them. There are legal fees and expenses paid to the birth mother. It is not like in the UK. These agencies simply do not exist here. Babies are so very rarely given up voluntarily for adoption in this country, and there is no monetary gain to be had for giving your baby up in the UK. Here the only babies and toddlers available for adoption are those who have been taken away from birth parents who find themselves in circumstances that prevent them from being able to look after their children as they would want to.

So I would need a lawyer over here to deal with visas and getting the baby over here, which would be expensive. I was looking at about $50,000 before I'd even started and I knew there would be more costs on top of that. I thanked the lawyer who had very patiently talked me through the process. There were a lot of questions unasked, but he had given me the answers I needed to be getting on with. The initial hope and giddiness of the phone call had turned into a feeling of panic, and something else I couldn't quite put my finger on.

I had no money; we had already established that when I had looked into surrogacy, but I telephoned the bank anyway to find out how much money I had just in case a miracle had occurred. I had very little: the cupboard was bare. There was no way I could afford this route. I looked down at my notebook. It was a mess of scribbles, doodles and numbers leading to nowhere. Again, had I given myself time and space to breathe, then maybe these options could have worked for me. But I didn't. And they couldn't. If I'd had the headspace to think logically, I could have got a loan, or done a well-paid acting job. There were options, even though they didn't seem to be apparent at the time.

But the truth is, deep down, I believe that the fact that I didn't make this happen truly means that it wasn't meant to be. As with most decisions in my life, just as I knew I wasn't pregnant with every failed attempt at IVF, in my gut I knew this wasn't my path. The feeling I couldn't put my finger on was guilt. It felt a bit like I was buying a baby and that didn't sit right with me. I didn't feel comfortable with the idea that there were women out there being paid, even under the guise of expenses, to give up their babies. Even then I knew that wasn't the same thing as a woman having to give up her child due to her life circumstances. Despite my desperation, I knew my conscience couldn't cope with that.

The road was narrowing very quickly. Looking back, I could cry for myself, this unrecognisable woman who was so obsessed and lost in this new and slightly more brutal reality. It was a world away from clean IVF clinics and lovely, smiling Dr Taranissi. It was a world where everything was above board, yes, but the boundaries were less clear and, frankly, if you had the money, anything was possible. I would like to take that broken woman and hold her hand, look into her eyes and reassure her that all would become clear. That it would all be OK.

At this point there were more roads closed to me than were open, but what was becoming evident was that adoption was a viable path. And, for the first time, the possibility of becoming a mother to a child who wasn't biologically mine genuinely didn't feel like second best.

I had to let go of all the things I had grown up thinking would happen. I had to let go of my imagined 'normal', of my vision of perfect, and get my head around my own kind of normal.

My mother had given birth to two girls and for years I had thought that I would just follow the same pattern, that it was the only way to be a mother. How wrong I was and how very glad I am now that I came to realise that. When I did let go of that vision, when I understood that you don't need to give birth in order to be a mother, it all seemed to fit into place.

It wasn't easy: I had to sit with it for a while, talk to people. I spent hours discussing it with my sister and my best friends. Victoria constantly found me uplifting stories of people who adopted. My best friend Angela confided in me that it was definitely something she dreamed about doing. I talked to them about how they viewed their children: did they always see their face staring back at them and did that make parenting easier? Or were their own flesh and blood sometimes completely unrecognisable to them? They all said it was a bit of both, but there were times they really didn't recognise their own children's behaviour, that they weren't exactly like them, that they couldn't always second-guess them. Sharing genes doesn't change that and I was gradually getting my head around the fact that a child not being like me didn't make me any less valid as a mother.

Once I had got over the mental hurdle and understood that I didn't have to grow a baby in order to love it, the world seemed to open up to me. It was liberating, to say the least. I could breathe again. I don't really know how this happened, other than it took time and a lot of conversations with as many people as would listen. Everywhere I went I searched for examples of people who had lived through a similar ordeal, trying the idea of adoption on for size again and again.

I received an amazing and heartfelt email the other day from a woman who had gone through four rounds of IVF and didn't know what to do next. She had reached the end of that road but was still desperate to become a mother and pretty sure that her successful career wasn't going to satisfy her on its own. She had been looking up 'infertility and moving on' on the internet and my name had come up. She asked me how

I had got over it: how had I moved on? How had I made the next step?

My honest answer is that I don't know. My ex-husband's wise words were definitely the catalyst; they moved the kaleidoscope so the pieces fell into a new place, but it was something I sat with and kept asking myself at different times of the day. Could I be a mother to a baby that wasn't home-made? The answer varied depending on the times I asked it. In the middle of the night alone in bed it was a definite no, but by the time I'd had a cup of tea and a chat with my sister after breakfast, it was a definite yes. I continued asking myself that question, day after day, over and over, until the answer was always a yes, until even when asked in the darkest hours the answer delivered was still: 'Yes.'

Your children are not your children.
They are the sons and daughters of Life's longing for
   itself.
They come through you but not from you,
And though they are with you yet they belong not to you.

Khalil Gibran

Chapter 8

I lay on my bed reading a book a friend had sent me called *Wuhu Diary* by Emily Prager. It was a book about a woman who adopted her baby from China and her journey to find out about her daughter's roots. It was a truly fantastic, heart-warming and inspirational book and I couldn't put it down. My plan was now well and truly adoption and I threw myself into it.

My mind started to spin and was filled with images of me adopting from China, travelling to the country with a suitcase of baby clothes for the child we hadn't met yet, but who was soon to be ours. Visiting orphanages and finding our daughter, picking her up and swinging her around and laughing in the sunshine, eating the food, visiting tourist attractions along the way and, ultimately, bringing her home. I could see the airport, full of well-meaning family and friends, ready to meet our daughter and welcoming us with open arms. I could almost smell her, she was so real. I loved the idea of the journey that I would go on. It all felt so exciting.

I immediately got on the internet and started googling Chinese adoption. At the time I couldn't find very much. There were a few links to actual orphanages and grainy pictures of little Chinese babies standing in cots. It was the early days of the internet, as I have said before, and there didn't seem to be a lot of information apart from a few pictures and the addresses of these orphanages. I couldn't just dial a number; I couldn't speak a word of the language for one thing and what would I say? How on earth was I going to start this journey?

As I scrolled through my searches, I finally found a number for a charity/agency that dealt with adoption abroad. Notebook and pen in hand (I had been here before), I dialled the number.

'Hello,' I said to the woman on the phone, 'I wonder if you could help me. I'm interested in adopting a baby from China.'

'OK,' said the slightly officious voice. 'Have you had your home study done?'

'No, I am at the very beginning of my journey. My husband and I are just starting to look into adoption. I have just read a book about a woman who adopted from China, and it's something we would really like to do.'

'Well, you would have to do some research on the country first.'

'What do you mean?' I said. 'I just want to adopt a child that needs a home.'

She sounded like she had heard it all before.

'Well, you have to start off with a project on China. We recommend you find out all you can about the country and its history. We also recommend that you start to learn Mandarin. There are plenty of courses, but you need to have a good grasp of the language. Then of course there's the money. To adopt a Chinese baby, it's about £12,000.'

'A project? Like a school project?'

'Well, yes, I suppose you could say that. You would be assigned a social worker and they will do a home study report on you. Then there are workshops we can sign you up to that will help you with your chosen country.'

'You can adopt from other countries as well?'

'Yes, India is about £8,000 and Russia about £10,000, though you have to look into things like foetal alcohol syndrome, as a lot of Russian babies have this. There are fees for home study reports and lawyers. There are lots of forms you need to fill in and you will need to get a social worker to assess you. If you're really interested I can send you some more information.'

'OK,' I said, wavering. 'You have given me a lot to think about. I'm not sure. I'll be in touch.'

I put the phone down and felt like I was in my very own Groundhog Day. The circumstances had changed slightly, but here I was, pad and paper in hand, with that overwhelming feeling that nothing is ever easy!

In front of me was a list of different countries and prices. To any stranger finding that piece of paper, it would have looked like a list of exotic holiday choices, not a catalogue for babies. Was this really what it had come to? I had finally got my heart into the right gear, only for my head to be bludgeoned by paperwork and bureaucracy. I knew that the whole process wasn't going to be easy, but I thought that I would feel joyful. I also thought that I would get a bit more support and have my hand held through the process. I didn't expect just to be bombarded with a whole load of scary information that didn't make any sense. I was mentally ready and had finally got myself to a place where I'd shut my body off from the whole process of having a child. Except now, I was overwhelmed in a different way.

I know it was only one phone call and an internet search, but it had completely floored me. I felt I had less power than ever before. This seemed worse than writing a letter selling myself to a surrogate. Essentially, I would have to do a school project and learn a new language and all I wanted to do was love a baby that needed a home. Could I really even contemplate learning Mandarin – not just a spoken language but a whole new alphabet? Did I really have any interest in China apart from wanting a cute baby and reading an uplifting book? Did I feel that pull in my gut that I had become so attuned to listening to? Did this feel right, like a thing me and my husband could do? The answer on the tip of my tongue to all of the above was no.

I felt nothing but exhaustion. I desperately wanted a child, but it seemed like a huge mountain to climb in order to get one. (Oh, if I only knew what was to come!) I shook my head as those feelings of powerlessness swept over me. Why is it that some people can have sex with a virtual stranger and get pregnant without giving it another thought? Why should I have to go back to school in order to just start the process of being a mother? Sometimes life seemed bloody unfair. I talked it through with my husband after the phone call and his face said it all. 'A project. On China?'

The other day, in the name of research, I looked up the agency I had spoken to and there was no longer any record of it online. However, there are now a few places that deal with intercountry adoption, along with easy-to-navigate websites and FAQs. All the information is there, and it feels much more personal; you get the sense that there may be someone who could actually guide you through it all. When I looked into this 15 years ago, it was a very different world and one that I really couldn't get my head around. I know this had a lot to do with the rather daunting person I spoke to on the phone, but also my body was probably still carrying hormones from far-away IVF cycles. I had been through so much mentally and physically in a relatively short period of time and, quite possibly, I hadn't given myself the time I needed to repair.

A lot of people go down the path of intercountry adoption and it is truly glorious. They become mothers and families and that is their path. It's all horses for courses: what at the time seemed to me like a daunting journey of drudgery fills other people with excitement and fuels their fire. They would tell me that for them it was all meant to be. And for them it was. We all get there in the end if we truly want to. From that one phone call and all the reading that was available to me via the internet, I knew that this wasn't my path. It's funny, that little thing called intuition. Your mind pushes you this way and that, throwing out all the ideas, but it's your gut that makes the decisions (or it's my gut anyway!).

The films of Chinese babies and incredible foreign journeys faded in my mind. This wasn't my story. And I was OK with that. What I did know was that I was ready to be a mother to an adopted child. I just needed to find my own way. I wasn't going to lose this feeling. It wasn't going to beat me. Some people would call me a dog with a bone, some people would call me mad, but I felt like Harry at the end of *When Harry Met Sally*. I had realised that I wanted to adopt and, when I realised that was my destiny, I wanted the rest of my life to start *now*.

I wrote in my diary at the time: 'It occurs to me that the most important thing – in fact the only thing – children need is constant, unconditional LOVE. We have lots to give. We can do this!'

During this time in my life I started confiding in family and friends again. I had become pretty secretive during the whole IVF process and then I had been on such a wild ride made up of so many different schemes that I had hardly had time to process each new thought. It was only now, when I had a firm idea in my head, that I felt able to talk openly and honestly with my sister again. She was so pleased that we were considering something that had a positive and sure outcome after the past few years of uncertain ups and downs. Trying for a child you couldn't conceive was crushing, whereas wanting to open our hearts and home to a child who needed love was a certainty – we knew there were children out there who needed that.

The more I talked about the possibility of adopting, the more real the idea began to sound. My godmother called me one day and told me she had a friend who lived down her road who had adopted a little boy and she would be very happy to talk to me about it. I took her number and excitedly gave her a call. This phone call has stayed with me ever since. I remember thinking I was going to get a lovely, friendly reception from this fellow adoptive mum, but it was completely the opposite. She was nice, but not warm: she wanted to tell me exactly how it was. She told me adoption was what she called 'parenting plus'.

'You have all the trials and joys and ups and downs of parenting, the usual day-to-day stuff, but with an adopted child there is always a plus', she said. 'There will be issues. There are always reasons as to why your child is acting a certain way. There will always be extra stuff you have to deal with and it's not pretty and doesn't fit into neat boxes.'

She got my back up almost immediately and I remember thinking, 'Yeah, yeah, you just want to shock me. I know that I will be all right because you obviously don't love your child as much as I'm going to love mine.' (Again, how little I knew!) At the end of the conversation, she asked me where I was thinking of adopting from. I told her that I had been looking abroad and she came right out and said, 'Why on earth aren't you thinking of England? There are thousands of children who need homes.'

I told her I didn't know, and that I would look into it. I just wanted to get off the phone as soon as possible. I didn't like the feelings that it had released in me. Maybe I was looking too far away, maybe what was staring me in the face was closer to home all along and I just hadn't realised it, like Dorothy in *The Wizard of Oz*. Why hadn't I thought of adopting from the UK? The simple answer is that I had heard horror stories of the adoption process taking years, that there were no babies put up for adoption and that children were taken away from their birth families because of dire circumstances, and that worried me.

I wasn't sure I could cope with a child's history that I had had no control over. In all honesty I knew nothing about the system here. I had thought adoption overseas would be easier, for some reason, possibly giving me a bit of distance from the whole process because there was a journey that went with it. The idea of adopting from abroad felt more like a film and less of a reality.

I decided to have a proper look into adoption from the UK and the first person I thought to approach was my doctor. I had seen posters for adoption and fostering pinned to the board in the surgery when I had visited her after the ectopic and for Clomid. She knew my need for a baby, for a family, and I thought she might be able to offer some advice. She told me to get in touch with my local authority, as they would be the first port of call. I rang and spoke to a person who was so full of doom and gloom I wondered how they got up every day.

'Where are you and your husband from and how old are you both?' was the first question.

'We are both British; I am 34 and he is 30.'

'So, do either of you come from any ethnic backgrounds?'

'No.'

'Well, I'm sorry but, although you are the right age, you will find it pretty impossible to adopt a baby through us. The majority of babies we have are from black or mixed-race parents and they don't get placed with white families.'

'What, so that's it? Even though we live in London which is a hugely diverse city, and have many close friends from different ethnic backgrounds, we can't adopt a child that is black or mixed race, because we are white?'

'Yes, that's currently the rule. Look, there is an adoption exhibition on for Haringey next week. You could go to that and see what options are available to you, but I don't think it will be your local authority.'

OK, an adoption exhibition.

A week later Chris and I made our way to the shiny new Arsenal stadium, to a big hall with lots of people milling about with stalls with banners above them saying 'Barnardos' and 'Coram' (adoption charities that I had no idea existed until then) and the names of various fostering agencies. I had no idea that adoption was so big; the idea that an exhibition could be held at a football stadium felt bizarre to me. We were both nervous and looked for a place to get a drink. We grabbed a lukewarm coffee from an urn and a couple of biscuits and surveyed the room. There were a lot of people who seemed a good few years older than us, all looking as uncomfortable as we were.

We sat down to listen to a speech that was just about to start. I recognised the guy on stage; we had worked together on a TV show years before. He talked about the fact that he was adopted by a white family in rural Oxfordshire in the 1970s. His mum and dad and siblings loved him, and he said that he had a pretty idyllic childhood and that he truly loved his family. But he said he always felt different, that his mum didn't know what shampoo to use for his hair or how to comb it. That there were no other black people in the village he grew up in. That love does conquer all but maybe it would have been more beneficial for him to have felt that he fitted in. That maybe, had he been adopted by a black family, he would have felt that he was more accepted.

I listened and argued in my head but, eventually, I understood what he was saying. In fact, what I wrote in my diary that night was: 'Suddenly what is staring us in the face is that it isn't all about us, and what we want, it is about the children. We have been of the mind that it doesn't matter where the baby is from, whether it's black or white or Asian, we would just love it and give him or her a good, loving, secure home. What we hadn't thought of is how the children would feel, how important it might be for them growing up to feel like they fit in. How it's important for the child to feel that they belong.' (Again, times have now changed, and it is much easier to adopt a child of any colour or ethnicity because, at the end of the day, love does conquer all. But I could see what this man was saying, and it was glaringly obvious.)

We looked at the stalls, chatted to a few well-meaning social workers who wanted to help us, but said that it was going to be difficult, and took leaflets from different agencies. The local authority stand did just send us away.

A little later on in the evening, a kindly social worker came up to us and said that she was very happy that we were considering adoption as there are a lot of children who need families. However, as we were both young and white, we would be better off going to a private agency like Barnardo's or Coram, if we didn't want to go abroad. She told us these agencies deal with social services and local authorities, but they also place children for adoption who are sometimes more difficult to house, due to drugs and alcohol issues. It was a lot to take in. We left clutching our leaflets, feeling a little despondent, but determined not to give up.

It's funny, but as soon as we had dipped our toe in the water, we discovered that a lot of people we knew had friends or friends of friends who had adopted, and we met some lovely people who were happy to share their experiences and their children's adoption stories with us. I think it really helped us just going to people's houses and seeing that their lives were completely normal.

As I've said, I had always had this image of adopters as properly religious types who made their own clothes, grew their own food and sung 'Kumbaya'. I had no true point of reference. It was either that image or Angelina Jolie and Madonna with their rainbow families and seemingly charmed lives. It was comforting to see that adopted children really were the same as birth children. Their parents drank wine and watched telly. They had arguments and shopped in Tesco; their houses were filled with plastic toys and cuddly teddies. They went to school, had friends, went on holiday, made Sunday lunch and were generally just parents.

It was beginning to feel normal. Yes, it was all a little daunting, but we felt for the first time in years that we were on the right road. Bolstering this feeling was the fact that things kept getting thrown in our path to help us along the way.

One of those things thrown into my path by the universe was Mary.

My agent at the time had a client who had adopted a child and she said she was sure he would speak to me if that would help. I got in touch and he sent me his wife's number and that's how I ended up sitting at Mary's kitchen table talking about adoption. Mary, like me, is an actress and I liked her immediately. She is one of the most warm, open and strongest people I had ever met. She told me her story and talked about the pros and cons of adoption, but she did it with a real honesty – not dressing it up to be an amazingly worthy and wonderful thing, but also not putting me off. She told me it straight.

She talked about meeting her baby and the love she felt, and how she was even thinking about adopting again. She wasn't a social worker or a 'good Christian woman', she was an actress, warts and all; she had a past. She was also on the telly and the adoption agency and social workers hadn't been put off by any of that. She lived in a house similar to mine; we knew the same sort of people. Meeting her, the wheels started to turn, to properly turn, that maybe this really was for me.

I looked around her warm kitchen, and truly identified with her surroundings and her words. She made me feel that I definitely had the strength to do this. She made it feel normal and lovely and not at all weird. I came away thinking that I could do what she had done. I could have my baby. She talked to me about Coram, the adoption charity they had found their daughter through. She told me that they had done something called concurrent planning. It is now called early permanence care and the Coram website describes it this way:

Concurrent planning is a specialist fostering and adoption service and a way of finding forever families for babies and young children aged up to three years. It ensures that every child is given stability and love from the start.

The scheme is for babies and young children who are in care and who are likely to need adoption, but who also still have a chance of being reunited with their birth family. While the birth parents are being assessed, concurrent carers initially perform the role of foster carer while the courts decide whether or not a child can return to its birth family.

During this time the child will see their birth parents regularly and the concurrent carers support the birth family's efforts to regain the care for their child.

If the courts decide that the birth family have shown they can be reliable, able and loving parents, the baby will be returned to their care. The concurrent carers will have the satisfaction of knowing that they have given the child the best possible start in life by providing care and security from the earliest time, and will play a part in helping them settle back into their family.

However, if the courts decide that the child's parents cannot provide the security and care they need, and there are no alternative carers from within the birth family, the child will remain with their concurrent carers and be adopted by them.

This was something I had never heard of before. It was different from straight adoption, but the key point was that it meant that babies or very young children were placed with these concurrent carers. So, if the birth parents couldn't look after that baby, it would have the security of staying with the foster family without all the disruptive moves that can come with children waiting for adoption.

It sounded hard but I knew it meant that we would be doing something good, caring for a baby and helping its little life in some way. After looking at all the paths we had gone down, after seeing price tags for babies and writing letters and feeling that it was all quite a selfish desire, this sat nicely with me. I wanted to be a mother, yes, but if I was going to help someone in the process, I would be even happier.

I know as I write this it seems like quite a big leap. First that we decided to adopt, and then that this other way, concurrent planning, was thrown into our path. Believe me, at the time I didn't really know exactly what it entailed but I knew somewhere deep down that this could be a real option for us. I wanted to find out more about it all, and I was excited.

I could really feel the sun starting to peek out from behind the clouds.

Eleven years on and Mary and I are firm friends. She is one of my rocks. We talk and text and walk and eat and can be honest in a way that not many people understand. After so long being scrutinised by social services and being the most PC person you can be, sometimes it's nice to just let rip, to say and feel the things you shouldn't say and know that you won't be judged and that it's all OK.

We sat together today and, after a long and heartfelt conversation about our daughters, I thought again about how very strong she is, how totally giving and, above all, how her relationship with her daughter is almost a mirror of mine. We love with a fierce love, all-consuming and completely selfless. She knows to go with the flow, that things are never how you planned and not much can be controlled. She has taught me to just go with it. To stop always trying to fix things. To just let go. And love. She is one of the best mothers I know.

Mary is the reason that I went on to adopt through Coram and the reason I thought I could do concurrent planning. Chris and I talked about it in more detail, and we both felt that this was the way forward for us. He was happy that I had found a way that I thought could work. He was pretty sure it sounded like a plan, so we called Coram to find out what would happen next.

Frequently Asked Questions
on Adoption

Is it going to take years and be a very intrusive process?
The adoption process does take a while but for good reason. We went to the open day at the beginning of January and were approved as adopters ten months later, so in reality, for us, it took as long as it does to grow a baby. It is intrusive in the fact that you are asked to dig deep into your personal life. You will be asked about situations in your past that may not be too comfortable to relive but all these things need to be addressed. If you think about it as a kind of therapy it definitely takes the pressure off.

Also it's worth remembering that all the hard things that may have happened to you in your past, including infertility, shape you into the person you are today. The very fact that you have dealt with them and come to terms with them equips you in some way to deal with the situations ahead. Social workers have to be thorough, they have to know about your family and friends and support network, they have to know about your health and financial situation, they need to see how you have coped in times of crisis – because you will be looking after a child that has been in very vulnerable situations. They need to know that you can keep that child safe and help him or her on their journey through life.

The waiting process can be tough once you have finally been approved. We waited only four months. Friends of mine waited six months, other people I know have waited eight months but most people have been matched within a year. I honestly think that your child finds you – but whether it's three months or three years, that wait will seem the longest of your life.

Is there support for the family supporting you?
There are workshops that are offered to friends and family of the adopters and they are truly worth going to. These workshops bust the myths and really help extended family gain a proper understanding of what it's like for the adopted child. It helps them realise that it is not about themselves or their family, it is always about the child. It also gives them tools to support you through the process.

Does it cost a lot?
When you foster a child you get an allowance. With adoption you don't; however, they do give you an allowance at the beginning to help you get started and there are benefits available. The workshops are free so you don't have to pay to attend but once your child is adopted they are yours and you support them financially as you would a birth child.

Will I love an adopted child like my own?
I can hand-on-my-heart, 100 per cent say that I love my daughter more than if she was my own. I couldn't have made

151

her more wonderful. My love is fierce and never-ending and unconditional, and every adopted parent I have met in my life says the very same thing.

Will an adopted child ever feel like my own?

Ownership is a big one, but the real question is: are our children ever our own? My daughter feels very much mine, but she doesn't belong to just me – she belongs to a huge family of people. I am blessed with the 'task' of taking care of her and loving and supporting her forever but as she gets older I share her with more and more people and I am happy with that. I would like to share her with the whole world because she shines so bright.

Do all adoptive children come with problems?

I think all people come with problems; it's very rare you meet someone who has had a charmed and blessed life. Everyone has hurdles. But yes, there will almost definitely be hills you have to climb. We are learning more and more about childhood trauma. The difficulty that comes with a lot of moves in a child's early life. Situations babies encountered *in utero* even have an effect. All I can say is that there is support out there. Friends with birth children have issues too and often say they wish they had the support we adopters have.

Where do you stand on nature versus nurture?

You have to be open to love every single bit of your child. Everything that made them and brought them to you. People will remark how alike me and my daughter look and that is because of the mannerisms she has picked up from me. There is stuff I know she has learned from me and stuff that is just inherent in her. A child can definitely be brought up to know what's right and wrong, and for the record I don't think anyone is born evil. I think we can get bogged down in nature and nurture; at the end of the day the fact is that they are who they are. We are all made up of many people that have shaped our lives, whether it be by blood or by example.

Can birth parents come and track the child down? Do I have to let my child have contact with their birth family?

Most adopted children have some form of contact with their birth parent(s), usually in the form of a letter every year. Some people have face-to-face contact. If there are adopted siblings there can also be sibling contact. As an adoptive parent you have a responsibility to help your child come to terms with their adoption and discussing their birth family is a huge part of that. Contact really does depend on the individual child as in some instances it is not safe and in others it is something that happens every year.

Contact with birth family will always have an effect on the child in some way. The more it is talked about the less it is something to be feared. You will always find advice and support on this from your local authority or adoption charity, and the older your child gets, the easier it is to talk to them about this. With social media it is much easier to track down birth family and vice versa (see the question below). The only way through this is by keeping those lines of conversation open between you and your child, so that whatever happens they can always talk to you and not be scared of how you are going to react.

What are the pitfalls of social media with an adopted child?
This is a relatively new area that affects your child when they get to secondary school and start using social media. It is a constant, ever-changing minefield. All I can say is that the more open and honest you are with your child and the more they feel that they can talk to you, then whatever happens with social media, at least you will know about it. There are many instances of adopted children contacting birth parents and vice versa even though legally they have to wait until they are 18. The difficulty is that in a lot of cases neither party is emotionally ready to deal with what happens next. Keep talking. It's the best way to keep your child safe.

Is there a support group that carries on helping you after the adoption?
There are many support groups. Good places to start are the websites first4adoption.org.uk and corambaaf.org.uk. However, you do find your own way. I think after you have adopted your child you sometimes need a little bit of time away from social services and support groups and workshops. Just to settle in and become a family in your own right. But don't be afraid to ask for help and use these groups when you need to. Honestly, it's amazing to feel that you are not alone when you are going through some issues.

That feeling of all eyes being on you from social services – does that ever stop?

Once all the visits are out of the way and your child is legally adopted I think it takes a while to stop feeling 'judged'. You do feel as if all eyes are constantly on you. But as you grow to know your child and trust your instincts it does eventually fade into the background and you do become their parent.

Does love really conquer all?

I am a great believer in love being the strongest connection. I do believe that love really can conquer all, though not without a great deal of patience and time and a good support network. But essentially all of this is brought about through love so … yes, I believe it does.

Chapter 9

When I decided that I wanted to write this book, I dug out my old diaries. They stopped around the time I underwent the IVF and started up again when we began our adoption journey. Funnily enough, they tailed off once more when we had adopted Billie and I was crazy busy being a mum. I have decided to use the entries in this chapter to paint a picture of the workshops and my thoughts at the time. What strikes me, looking back, is that I used these diaries as a way of giving myself the 'pep talks' I needed. It was as if writing my thoughts down meant they would manifest themselves and come true. They take me straight back to the time and are a combination of complete honesty and hope for what might be. A bit like *Field of Dreams* ... if you write it, it will come.

Coram had an open evening coming up and Chris and I called and put our names down. Both of us were really nervous as we pulled up outside the campus and we were only going to an open day. The car journey there had been fraught, you could practically hear my brain whirring with questions and thoughts and I was wound up about anything and everything:

traffic, red lights, learner drivers, all put in our path seemingly deliberately and making me panic that we were going to be late. I had hardly eaten that day, I was so consumed with the open evening and what it would mean to us. We hadn't even signed anything yet, just expressed an interest! I have to admit I felt scared. What were we thinking?

We parked and took a deep breath. I put on my 'big girl pants' and forced a smile. Let's try to look at this as exciting not scary, I thought to myself. We were led towards a red-brick building and into a dull, grey room filled with chairs. About 20 people milled about, congregating around the urns for tea and coffee and plates of biscuits. Before we had a chance to run, two women clapped their hands and welcomed us all. We found a couple of chairs and I got my notepad out.

The meeting was great. The women explained the difference between general adoption and concurrent planning, going into detail about how it worked. Basically, with straight adoption the child has already been in foster care and through the courts and is waiting to be placed with a family. Adoptive parents very rarely get to meet the birth family and the children are usually aged from about two upwards. With concurrent planning, or early permanence care, babies or very young children are placed with foster carers that have already been approved as adopters. If the courts decide the baby cannot be looked after by the birth family, then the foster carers/adopters get to keep the child. What this means is that there is more continuity of care for the child. It will either stay with those carers or go back to a birth parent who has been assessed.

Concurrent planning can obviously be very hard for the carers as the baby may not stay with them and they may have started to form a bond with that child. However, they would have the comfort of knowing that they had given that child complete stability in a very unstable situation. Ultimately if a baby can stay with its birth parent that is the best solution and as long as the carers know that then it is a system that works well.

It's really important to point out here that, although we were told this over and over, it was something I really had to dig deep to find within myself. The statistics of children in care going back to birth parents is extremely low (depending on individual circumstances) but I knew what it was like to draw the short straw statistically, being the only person in my IVF round who didn't fall pregnant. Statistics meant nothing and I had to be at peace with the fact that the child could go back to its birth parent. I had to truly believe that if that were to be the case it would be in the child's best interest. And that was bloody hard. To come all this way, still desperate to be a mother, and then to have to arm myself with the possibility of not keeping the child … it was no easy feat. After all I had been through, I don't know why I thought I could do this – but there was something deep in my gut pulling me on, saying 'yes you can'.

The two women at the front definitely took on the role of good cop and bad cop and almost tried to put us off the whole experience. They really told us how it would be, but Chris and I came away thinking that this was really something that we could do. We went away with a questionnaire to fill in and a number to call if we wanted to take it further and arrange a meeting.

We got back in the car and, unlike the charged silence of the journey there, the way home was filled with conversations about how we felt that we could do this. We were both surprised that we felt the same way, that, although it seemed properly hard, it also seemed worth it. This was definitely something we wanted to explore further. Maybe it was the way the social workers talked about our options, so clearly and honestly, or maybe something had shifted in both of us after the long, dark days behind us. Either way, we both felt ready to begin this journey.

That night I wrote in my diary: 'The thought of "giving up" six months or so to foster a baby and give it the best possible start, whether it stays with us or not, seems like a great and unselfish thing to do. Let's face it, after all that IVF, life becomes self-absorbing and we would like to try and help a child.'

Never one to let the grass grow under my feet, I called the next day and arranged a meeting with a lovely social worker who told us she thought we would be great candidates for concurrent planning. She was patient and kind with us and listened to our story and what had led us to Coram. She was super positive about the whole adoption process, while all the time making sure she was being fair and honest. The next steps, she said, were to enrol on a four-week group workshop. In the meantime, she advised that we read a book called *Adopters on Adoption*.

I wrote in my diary: 'It has certainly started preparing me for what's to come. Some days I feel quite daunted by the whole prospect. But most of the time I feel excited. I'm not sure what these workshops are going to be like – although I'm an actress, I hate standing up and talking about myself! Also, will there be right and wrong answers to everything? Will we get through these first stages? I'm so looking forward to learning about all this. It's scary but exciting and as Chris pointed out it's the beginning of our "weird" pregnancy.'

The day of the first group workshop arrived and again we were very nervous. I had, as usual, worked myself up into a bit of a frenzy and was dreading it. Fear of the unknown, sure, but also I knew I would learn things that I didn't want to hear about – painful stories that would become par for the course. Would I be strong enough to deal with it all? Would I be good enough?

I took a deep breath and opened the doors to the next stage of my life.

We were greeted by the two social workers running the programme, who were very friendly and open. Our minds were put completely at rest when we met the other people on our course. There were about six other couples and a woman on her own. There was that weird thing that always happens around a tea and coffee urn. People congregate around it and pour manky tea and coffee into Styrofoam cups and take biscuits that they would never normally eat. I think it's a form of comfort. Everybody's in a weird situation, having an almost out-of-body experience, drinking and eating things they would usually complain about. It has the feel of a hospital waiting room or a teachers' staff room. There's a sort of familiarity about it that makes you feel safe. So as we poured ourselves tea and munched on biscuits, we all realised we were in the same boat; we were all nervous and none of us knew what to expect.

What struck me was that everybody seemed pretty normal. Nobody was in dungarees and a knitted hat, everyone seemed professional and youngish. Later, I wrote in my diary: 'I don't really know what I'd define as "normal" but when we signed up for all this, I think we had a preconceived idea that people would be very different from us.' I think that's a lot of people's preconception. That nobody who adopts is normal. That you have to be a bit odd to want to do it. I am here to assure you lots of people think that way and to promise you that it's really not true. Most of the group were just like us: youngish, with a huge desire to be parents and give a child a loving home. So my judgements stopped there.

We were all given a sticker with our name on it and our first task was to go up to someone, introduce ourselves and tell them something about our name, why we were called it, what it means, did we like it, etc. I decided to dive straight in and break the ice for everyone else. I went up to a woman and introduced myself. The reason I am called Lisa is that my mum said that if I was a girl then my dad could choose my name. He was a massive Elvis fan and his daughter is called Lisa Marie, so he named me after her. I said that my mum had never liked my name and thought it was 'common' but that I had always really liked it, apart from when people pronounce it wrongly, adding a 'z' instead of an 's', which drives me up the wall!

This was a really good ice-breaking exercise and initially that's what I thought it was, but the reason behind it was to see how important names are. Sometimes the only thing that an adopted child has from its birth parents is its name and so it is extremely important to keep it. I hadn't ever considered this before. It all made great sense.

After the first exercise we had all begun to relax a little and we threw ourselves into the next tasks. The social workers made it so easy and the group was alive with conversation and even a bit of laughter.

We were then given an example of a case study of a three-year-old girl called 'Sarah'. We were told that, after a lot of visits from social workers and eventually the police when she was left home alone, she had to be removed from her birth mother's care. She went to live with a foster family and started to thrive but the foster mother had an accident and so she was moved to another foster family that already had a three-year-old and things were quite difficult. She was waiting all the while to be adopted and finally found a forever family that same year. The birth mother's social worker, the child's social worker and the local authority were all involved in the wellbeing of little Sarah, as well as the foster carers and birth parents and adopters.

We were asked to do what was called a 'sculpt', a sort of still life or tableau of Sarah's situation and all the people around her. I volunteered to be Sarah and sat in a chair at the centre of the room. Meanwhile, other people took on different roles and we soon had a tableau of all these people bearing down on this little girl. It was amazing to see how many were actually involved in the whole adoption process. We were all asked to try to articulate how we felt, being the person we were playing. I said that I felt anxious and confused about being taken away from my mother and then because I had moved again and again I would try to just keep quiet and blend into the background in an attempt to be able to stay where I was.

Although it sounds like one of those horrid team-building trust exercises you hear about, it was actually fascinating, hearing from each other's points of view and understanding how all the different people would be feeling. How difficult it must all be for the birth mother and how much patience and love and care Sarah would need, and also how much support the adoptive parents might need too. I felt like I had found my people; we all understood each other and the tough journey ahead for all concerned. These exercises were absolutely integral to us seeing adoption from all sides. We could have talked about it for hours, there seemed so much to say, but our time was up and it was over for another week.

We all came away from the first session feeling quite relieved and bloody exhausted. It felt lovely to get out of the hot, stuffy room and into the cold night air. I took great big gulping breaths. I felt exhilarated but sad at some of the feelings that had been brought up at this first meeting. I wrote in my diary:

'Relieved that we have finally made a start on this long journey. Everyone seemed so nice and I am actually looking forward to next week. Something that I never thought I would say.'

My diary entries over the next few weeks record the highs and lows of the process:

Tuesday 20 February 2007

I decided when I started to write this adoption diary that there was no point if I wasn't going to be honest. I'm feeling really low about it all today. I know that none of it is helped by the fact that my wonderful grandad died last week and his funeral was yesterday. I miss him already. Even though these last few months he had hardly spoken, sometimes I would just look in his eyes and for a minute I would see him and know that he saw me – that he still saw me and knew I was there.

I just feel a bit swamped by it all. The workshop on Monday was about adopted children's feelings towards adults by the time they are adopted, how they view them and also the problems that may arise. For example, your child is caught stealing pencils/lunch money from someone at school. How do you deal with this? We all agreed that this scenario may have nothing to do with a child being adopted and could happen to any child, but we would have to be sensitive as it could be a result of your adopted child's past. Maybe they feel that they didn't have anything and it might be taken away again or they need some sort of attention, any attention, so that they don't get forgotten. All sorts of reasons.

We also looked at life story books. This is a book that an adopted child has to explain where they came from. It generally features photos of their birth parents and a very simple age-appropriate explanation of why they couldn't look after them. It includes photos of foster carers, maybe photos of the child with their favourite toy. Then pictures of their adoptive parents and forever family. It is a little 'bible' so that children can get to grips with how they got here and who they are. Our homework is to make up a life story book using a case study they have given us. It is all fascinating, a lovely exercise to do and extremely helpful, but I just feel sad. Sad that these poor children will feel different because they are adopted when they have been through so much already. Sad that we have to go through this difficult process in order to have a baby. Scared that I won't live up to all this, that I won't be able to handle it, that our child will resent us. Angry that it isn't 'easy'. Upset that this child won't have any of my genes, that my grandad's eyes won't shine through theirs.

I know, or I think, that these are all normal feelings you go through on this journey, and I also know how worthwhile it will all be. But sometimes, like today, it all feels like an uphill struggle.

I so want to have a house full of toys and noise and love. I love children so much.

I don't feel scared about adoption; I feel confident it's the right way to go. Maybe these feelings would come to the surface if I were pregnant naturally, doubting my ability to be a good parent ... ?

Tuesday 27 February

What a lot can change in a week!

Last night's workshop was great. We had two adopters come in and talk to us about what it was really like. They were lovely. I'm constantly struck by how 'normal' these people are. They said they were envious of us all, how exciting the journey was and told us just to enjoy it. And I thought 'yes!' This *is* all enjoyable and something I must remember. It goes so fast. They told us the highs and lows. How they got their child. Troubles with him now and support groups that were helping them. They seemed so relaxed about it all, and I felt much better after listening to them. Basically I feel like I should try to enjoy every minute of this process, the ups and the downs. It seems like Coram are really supportive; I think there will always be someone to help. I also feel with concurrent planning that if we don't get to keep the baby then at least we will have known what it was like to have a baby in the house: sleepless nights, nappies, feeds, etc. And how wonderful really if the birth parent gets it together to look after their child.

Then we will have helped its start in life. I like that thought.

I love that I can see how my mindset had started to shift here. That I liked the thought of helping a baby. Truly it was such a joy to be thinking about others. It was nice to feel that I was part of a bigger process that wasn't at all self-centred. Anyone who has gone through a struggle to have a baby will understand what I mean by feeling so self-absorbed. Your whole world becomes quite tiny and suffocating and all you really ever think about is yourself and how it's all affecting you. It felt truly refreshing to see things a different way. To feel that we could do something that would help us and help a child at the same time.

The angry struggles I had experienced had waned. But that's not to say I was always at peace with it all. On my dark days (and there were still many) I berated myself for taking this journey. I couldn't understand why I would put myself through this and I'm sure as you read this you may be thinking the same. What an uncertain way to become a mother – I obviously liked pain! I can only say in my defence that it was lovely to feel that I had a plan and a process that would have an end result. Whenever I wavered there was someone I could talk to who would pull me back and help me see things more clearly. There was support, of which on reflection there was none going through IVF. I could pick up the phone to a social worker or talk to a fellow 'adopter' in a workshop, or call my friend Mary and we would have a patient and honest discussion. I was always asking myself the question of whether I had the strength to do this and most if not all of the time I found the answer was yes.

Thursday 8 March

We had our last workshop this week. I was quite sad to finish in a way.

We were split into two groups and we went off to read and discuss our life story books. There were only three couples in our group and we were last. Everyone had done theirs slightly differently and they were all really lovely.

I actually quite enjoyed doing the book, thinking about what we would put in it. I bought a couple of baby magazines and Chris got some photos off the internet; he said he felt really dodgy downloading pictures of random families but it was all in a good cause! It was quite difficult not to think of it as a school project and it is weird to think that at some point we will actually have to make a life story book for our own child. That's a whole different ball game to the task that we were set. I don't know, I just think you would want to make it really special for them. It's a big responsibility.

After we read the story books we had a talk about the 'handover' of children from the foster carers to you. How much time you would spend with the child once you had been chosen as the adopters, and what happens when you take them home. It's between about five and ten days of visits with the foster carers before you can take the child home, which is not very long. We've been told it's important to spend different times of day at the foster carers' home. I thought, 'What an upheaval for these children – they settle into a foster family then have to move again and learn to trust a load of new people.' No wonder some of these children have emotional problems. It does make me think we are going the right way with concurrent planning because at least the child gets a more stable start in life.

We also talked about filling in the adoption application form, which we now need to do. Bloody hell, that's a minefield. There's loads of stuff to fill in, all about what sort of child we would consider and our support network of people.

Lots of things to discuss and think about. I know I just have to break it down into little pieces but it did kind of throw me and I wish that someone could fill it in for us.

Chris and I discussed this form at length and I would like to say we were completely open-minded about every condition listed. However, we were not. When you get this form to fill in you *have* to be honest. You have to know what you can and can't deal with and, although it feels as if you are rejecting babies with all sorts of difficulties, ultimately it's the right thing to do. It would be far worse to have to give a child back if you realised you couldn't cope with a deformity or brain damage. It's a horrid form to fill in and it's something we put off as long as possible. There is no easy way around it and honesty really and truly is the best policy here. You cannot and must not worry about how the powers that be will judge you because they won't, I promise.

What we decided was that we didn't mind if we had a girl or a boy. I was adamant when I was pregnant for that short amount of time that I was having a boy. I could only see myself with a boy, which is funny as I had grown up with girls everywhere! But at this point, a relatively healthy baby, girl or boy, was the only thing that mattered. Goalposts shift as you make your way along the path and you make choices you would never have dreamed of before. You are asked to consider whether you would take a child with an unknown past, or a product of rape, one with a facial disfigurement or family history of schizophrenia. These are the dark days where you really wonder how you ended up here, filling in a form like this, and I have to say that without the odd bit of dark humour and like-minded people on the courses I think you would run a mile, and no one would blame you if you did. It's not meant to be easy and the people who stay the course are properly hardcore. Still on certain days 11 years on, I don't know how I managed it.

Sunday 18 March: Mother's Day

Will I finally be a mother this time next year? I wish my mother were here to help me.

Sometimes I get scared because when I'm with other people's children who I love dearly, and they need so much attention, I think can I really do this? It's hard enough looking after your own child that you have made. Or will my adopted child simply be mine as soon as it's in my arms?

Are these fears normal?

It's in this entry I see my yearning is still there. I was asking myself honest questions that I think every mother-to-be (birth or otherwise) would ask themselves. Could I really be a mother? This thing I wanted with all my heart. I was so close I could feel it and with that came all the last-minute panic of 'can I really do this?' I smile now as I read it, seeing the scared little girl that was inside me then and the mother I have become today.

Tuesday 27 March

We had our concurrent planning intense workshops this weekend. Our journey is at times quite weird and at times quite lovely.

There were seven of us in the group but no one from the adoption workshops we had done before. Two social workers took the group again, one being good cop and the other being bad cop. One was all smiles and positivity and the other was telling us like it is.

The first day we went through the differences between fostering and adoption and we did two 'sculpts', one with the child going to the concurrent carers and one with it going back to its birth mother. What was fascinating again was all the people involved and how it could so easily go either way and that either way the child feels secure and benefits.

There was a lot of discussion about the child going back to birth parents and the win/win situation for a child in concurrent planning, and what an important part we would have played in that child's life if that's the outcome.

We came away feeling exhausted. There is so much to take in and you spend so much time trying to always be the good person and to think fairly, and that's not always easy. Sometimes I just wanted to scream at the unfairness of it all and I wanted to take a walk around the block to still my beating heart, to always try to bring it round to the child and not myself.

The next morning we were hit with the health issues. Even though we knew them and had gone over them at every turn, it was very hard hearing it all again. Hep B and C, HIV. Mental illness, foetal alcohol syndrome, enough information to have you walking out the door quick smart! It is all very depressing, but once you break it down it's not that bad – well, that's what I'm hoping.

We were put into groups and had a discussion about what our biggest worry was. We were split into men and women and it was great talking to three other women who all felt the same as me. We all sort of bonded on that discussion and amazingly had the same worries and thoughts. We were also in agreement that all we really wanted for our children was for them to be able to have loving relationships and have friends and be happy.

After all this, a concurrent carer came in to talk to us. She was a welcome relief, so positive with a lovely story to tell. I think all of us felt after talking to her that this was finally within our grasp, that this really could be us sitting there in a year or so.

What strikes me about these diary entries is how after so many months of ups and downs and panic and not seeing things clearly, here I was sounding so calm about everything. How the hell did I go from manic to Zen in such a relatively short time? I almost seem like a different person. I wasn't, of course; all those mad feelings and worries were still whirring away but there was a definite shift and I used my diary as a sounding board. I think the human spirit has an amazing capacity to tell itself whatever it needs to in order to survive, and I needed to see that I could do this. I needed to see it written down in black and white, almost testing myself to see how those words sat with me. Did I really have the mental strength to love and help a child in the constant knowledge that it may not be forever? The more I wrote it, the more I believed it. Does that make sense? I thought about what was being told to me in workshops and for the first time in ages I really listened. It had been so hard for me to get to this point in my life and yet here I was. I was finally giving myself the time to get my head around every bit of the process, something I hadn't ever really done before. I had to surrender myself in a different way, to be almost passive.

I also kept thinking back to my meetings with Mary. Sometimes it takes just one person reframing the conversation to make you really see that you can do something. Mary had done it. She was proof it could happen, she was all I needed to be able to jump in with both feet.

Ironically, looking back on all this, I see it was the perfect preparation for the mindset I would need to have for raising an adopted child. They come with a 'cast' of their own important extended family and you share 'ownership' of the child you raise. That's the fundamental difference between being an adoptive parent and a biological one. There are so many more people than just you and it's a massive consideration, one that I had slowly and steadily got my head around. And looking back there was a reason that the courses were all so spaced out, to give you time to digest everything in between. You needed that period to be measured and calm and find the 'grown up' inside you that you would need for the very grown-up world ahead.

After the workshops we waited a few weeks to be assigned our social worker to carry out our home study report. Again another lot of waiting, but I had by this point got used to it. I knew I had to keep busy and not let myself spiral back into panic. We went on holiday and enjoyed just being a two. We were finally on our road, but there was a definite next stage to look forward to, which made it better.

A home study goes through everything. Your past, jobs, relationships, lifestyle, childlessness, parents – everything you could think of, basically. It's not easy and it made everything else that had gone before seem like a walk in the park. You meet once a week every week with your social worker and just talk. It's like therapy.

I was very excited to start our home study as it felt like we were really in it now. At home we were going about our daily life and I felt reasonably stable for the first time in years. I could talk to people normally; I had a purpose and I have to say that felt great!

However, our first meeting with our social worker didn't quite go to plan. I was nervous and excited and of course it didn't live up to expectations. How could it when I had built it up so much in my head?

We arrived at Coram, the red-brick building becoming more and more familiar to me, and I remember I desperately needed a wee. There was one loo in the building and I tried the door and it was locked. When it opened, 'Bad Cop' from the first ever meetings came out. We had talked about her in the car on the way home from the workshops saying how she had really played the part well and here she was standing in front of me.

'Bad Cop' was to be our social worker.

I smiled and went to shake her hand, but it wasn't exactly the best place to meet your social worker. She looked down at my hand and mumbled something about her hand being wet and left me hanging. This couldn't get much worse.

I composed myself in the loo when she had left, took a deep breath and went to meet her properly. We sat across the table from her in silence. She smiled but said very little. She asked us how we felt the workshops had gone and why we wanted to adopt. Both of us were understandably nervous of saying the wrong thing, and it all felt pretty excruciating. Let's just say she didn't put us at ease! She gave us some homework to do, which was to draw a diagram of our support network of people and their ethnicity. When it was time to leave she got up to show us out and I thanked her and (stupidly) went to shake her hand again to say goodbye. Witheringly, she took it. I was mortified and made a mental note not to shake hands with her in the future.

I left feeling worried. All the people I had spoken to said that their social worker had become a real friend and that they couldn't have got through the process without them. This looked like it definitely wasn't going to be the case with me. I tried to make myself feel better – maybe she was having a bad day, we all have them. Maybe next week would be better.

The weeks went by and things did improve. Our social worker thawed a little towards us and after a few sessions as a couple it was time to have our one-on-ones. Beforehand, I'd had to complete the homework of listing all of the jobs I'd ever had. As an actress you can imagine I had had many jobs, acting and non-acting. Trying to remember employers and how long the jobs were, etc. was no easy task and I cast my mind back to those heady days of thinking that a project on a country seemed the hardest thing I would have to do. Here I was digging deep and it was tough! There is so much paperwork. I'm not the most organised of people and to try to find all this information, bearing in mind I had been working since I was 17 years old, was a nightmare.

I met our social worker for our single session after lunch one afternoon. I think I talked solidly for two hours. We discussed my school, jobs, loads about my mum. I was annoyed with myself as of course I ended up crying and I didn't want it to seem like I was weak or hadn't dealt with 'stuff' in my past. It felt strange to talk about myself for so long. I know the old joke about the fact an actor likes nothing more than to talk about themselves but in reality when you are trying to be honest but also not say the 'wrong' thing it's pretty painful.

I came away feeling a little warmer towards her but I couldn't stop replaying the conversations in my mind. Did I say the right thing? Was she going to judge me for my alternative, slightly bohemian lifestyle? I certainly had a past and I didn't know if that would work for or against me. In the end I consoled myself with the fact that if I hadn't said the right thing then it wasn't meant to be. I had to leave it in the hands of fate or I would drive myself mad and I was just beginning to feel sane again. Amazing at the ripe old age of 35 I was finally growing up!

The next session was on childlessness and past relationships. I wrote in my diary: 'We got through it and I didn't cry! I thought I would because of the whole ectopic and IVF but it was OK. Our relationship with our SW [social worker] is much better now and I didn't feel quite so much that she was judging me. Also I think I've reached a point where I am who I am and if that's not good enough in their eyes then what can I do about it? Nothing. Came away feeling strong.'

I could feel each week I was changing. There were so many ups and downs, moments when I didn't want to think about adoption any more in case my brain exploded, moments when I couldn't get enough of what lay ahead, reading books and constantly questioning myself. The week after we explored the subject of 'childlessness' came the session where we discussed 'what sort of parents would we be?' Usually at this stage a lot of people do parenting courses but luckily my sister had always let me have the girls on a regular basis. I had been changing nappies, feeding them, bathing them and generally playing mum/auntie since the day they were born. It's all very different living it day in day out but it was one course we didn't have to attend!

We also had to fill out that form on what sort of child we would look at adopting. I touched on this earlier and it sounds as awful as it is. Basically it's a list of symptoms a child could have and what we would consider taking on. Things like facial deformities, Downs syndrome, FASD (foetal alcohol syndrome), ADHD, a history of schizophrenia or mental illness. It all makes for truly depressing reading if I'm honest and I spent a lot of time researching and calling friends or acquaintances who were doctors and teachers to ask them the reality of behavioural problems and mental illness. What was really important was that we were honest about what sort of child we could take on and we had to do a lot of soul searching. In the end we decided we would be happy to take on more issues than we first thought. Research is a must but we came to feel that you never know really what problems you may encounter with a birth child so why would it be any different if you're adopting? We had to try to make light of such a grim situation, saying that even if our child couldn't walk or talk or do anything we would just love them and wheel them around smiling. You have to remember that, for all the workshops and counselling, fundamentally I was still desperate to become a mum and we were desperate to be parents!

During this time of home study/'therapy', our friends and family were being seen and interviewed by our social worker. We weren't allowed to be there – anything they had to say about us was confidential and that was pretty scary. We chose my sister and her husband and my best friend Angela and her husband Jason as our referees. These were people who knew us better than anyone, who were willing to vouch for us being good parents but also to raise any concerns they had. I remember talking to both Ange and my sister about what they would say and both told me not to worry. They thought I would make the best mum in the land and they would be sure to let my social worker know. I made sure to tell them not to shake hands!

After weeks of meetings with our social worker it was time for her to write up her report on us and send it to the panel. This is where we would get approved as foster carers and adopters. (If and when we got the chance to adopt then we would have to go to another matching panel.) This was the first major hurdle we had to get over. Our first panel date was put back because the social worker's report on us wasn't ready. It was quite a blow as we were on tenterhooks just waiting to know when it would happen. It's so frustrating when you have done all you can do, attended all the courses, completed all the homework, filled in every form and you are just waiting for other people. Finally, we got a call a month after the original date.

Panel day dawned and again we were nervous as hell. I knew I had done all I could, that we were fully prepared for whatever questions the panel may ask but it was still scary and my heart was pounding so much I was pretty sure you could see it through my jumper! We walked into a room filled with about a dozen people, including our social worker and another social worker from Coram. Everyone else was independent, ranging from people who were adopters or had themselves been adopted to foster carers, family and child social workers and family lawyers and doctors. They put us at ease straight away; there was no good cop/bad cop going on here, just warm faces and an interest in what we had learned and what sort of parents we would make.

We answered all the questions they put our way. The whole thing took less than an hour. That feeling of being interviewed to see if you will make a good parent is unimaginable. Here you are after doing months of workshops and 'therapy' sessions, you have talked your way around every situation you may ever encounter as an adoptive parent – and then 12 people have the power to decide whether your greatest wish will be granted. That decision is all in their hands. It's exciting and nerve-wracking in equal measure. The sweat was running down my back – I felt hot and bothered and physically sick. What if they thought we weren't right? All the past few months would have been for nothing. This really, truly would be the end of the road.

We left the meeting room and our social worker came out a few minutes after. She told us that it was all looking good but that they had to formally talk about it and she would call later. We knew in our heart of hearts that, if we hadn't been ready to be adopters, if our social worker had any doubts, she probably wouldn't have taken us to panel. She was a taskmaster and for good reason.

About ten minutes after we arrived home, we got the call. I wrote in my diary:

We are approved as adopters!!!! Yay! Yay! Yay! We are over the first hurdle. We have done it. We are going to be parents. We don't know when but we know we will be. The best day!

My teacher is this bright eyed, big hearted little boy.
My school is the twisty turny world of foster care,
motherhood and life as a whole. And my church is all
of it. The deep breaths, the tears and the wild abandon
from which my heart loves you and learns to love all
of it.

Mary Beth LaRue

Chapter 10

A few months later my hugely pregnant best friend Nicola and I were Christmas shopping on Marylebone High Street. This was a place I had spent a lot of time walking up and down while waiting for IVF appointments, as it was a few minutes' walk away from the clinic. It is a beautiful street at the best of times but at Christmas there is something magical about it, with all the twinkling lights and luxurious shops. I felt happy to be walking arm in arm with my friend, sipping from our Starbucks red cups and excitedly chatting about me being her birth partner in the new year.

We had just walked into the Emma Bridgewater shop and were looking at pie dishes when my phone rang. It was Chris. He told me that Coram had just called. I hurried outside and left Nicola umming and aahhing.

It was freezing and the sky was nearly dark as I listened intently to my husband on the other end of the line. There was a baby. A little girl. Actually a little older than the usual concurrent babies – she was 17 months old. But they thought we would be a good match.

'Yes,' I said. 'What's her name?'

'Well, they are not usually meant to tell you names but she said it's Billie.'

'Yes,' I said again. 'Yes.' This was one of my original ideas for a name for a boy years ago in those heady days of planning babies naturally. It was also an abbreviation of my grandad's name, William. This was fate.

'Oh my God. Oh wow, is this really happening? Shall I call Coram back?'

'Yes, give them a call and then we can talk about it.'

Nicola by this point was standing at my side, desperate to hear the news.

'There's a baby,' I said. 'Well, a little girl actually. They wondered if we may be interested in meeting them to talk about her.'

The world seemed to slow down. Everything ground to a halt and sped up all at the same time. I needed to call Coram for myself and hear what they had to say. I needed to get home. We abandoned our shopping trip and hotfooted it to the car. My mind was racing. Could this really be it?

I dropped Nic home and rushed through my front door, impatient to speak to Chris about the baby. What did he think? Should we meet the social workers and find out more?

'Yes' was his immediate answer. We were both very conscious of not getting too excited but after so long the butterflies in my stomach were fluttering uncontrollably.

We spoke to the social worker at Coram and she gave us a little more information. They arranged for Billie's social worker to come to our house to talk to us. She had seen us on paper, as it were; she had read our file and we sounded like a good match, but she obviously needed to meet us in person and ask us questions, to see the house and get a feel of who we really were.

A week later we were opening the door to her. I had made biscuits and tidied the house, lit candles and then blown them out, thinking about fire hazards and child safety even though she was an adult coming alone. I was so scared of giving the wrong impression. Chris had tidied the garden and we had blocked the little pond at the back and were in the process of making it into a sandpit. We were both understandably nervous. This could be the decider on us becoming parents. What would she think of us? Would we be a good match?

We needn't have worried about being nervous. As soon as we met the social worker she gave us a massive smile and put us at ease straight away. We sat and talked about Billie, about what she was like. She showed us a photo of a super cute little girl with bright green eyes and a cheeky grin. She looked like a little pixie. We were already smitten. I didn't want to look at it too much but I couldn't tear my eyes away from the photograph. This little girl could potentially be our daughter, or at the very least someone we could look after and help.

The social worker asked us questions about ourselves, our jobs, our support network and the other children in our life. We felt confident answering the questions, happy that we had such a lot of experience with our nieces and godchildren. She told us there and then that she thought we would be a great match. She said she would like us to meet with Billie's foster carers as the next step. I asked if we could keep the photo and she said yes. That photo was never far from my person from that day on, clutched in my hands or safely between the pages of my diary in my handbag or standing up on my bedside table. Those little eyes so bright. We put in diary dates to meet with the local authority and foster carers and waved goodbye.

This was becoming more and more real by the day and soon after we met with Billie's foster carers. The local authority and Coram were all on board and the next step was to find out about Billie herself and work out a plan to meet her and bring her home.

We met up with Billie's foster carers one afternoon in December – Billie herself wasn't present at this point. I had a list of questions in a little notebook and I have to say I was terrified. Meeting another set of people who could possibly judge you is never easy and, even though we were getting used to it, being in a situation like this was never easy and I always felt like a schoolgirl going into these meetings. I had to remember this wasn't about me, that I was completely capable and had been approved as an adopter. We had attended all the workshops and groups; we had children in our house more often than not. We needed to prove nothing except that we would care for this child. And we weren't on trial here – this was just a meeting with the foster carers. They were there to help us.

They were lovely. We met with them and all the social workers involved. They told us Billie's routine and I have notes in my book about what washing powder they used, what bedding she had, what creams were used on her skin and what food she liked to eat. I wrote everything down, making a mental note to go to the supermarket on our way home to pick all these things up.

We were told that we must copy the routine she had with the foster carers pretty much to the letter so that she wouldn't feel that absolutely everything had changed. She had had a lot of moves and she needed to feel settled and safe. We were also told not to wash any bedding that she came with for at least a week so that everything still smelled the same for her at night. I totally understood how that sense of smell can have such an effect on you – I just have to smell a roast chicken in the oven and am immediately transported back to my childhood home and my mum's kitchen – so, although part of me wanted to buy all brand new, it made total sense to wait. That part would come.

The plan was that we would make a little picture book for Billie with photos of us and her new bedroom and house. It would just contain a handful of pictures that the foster carer could show to her every night. She was only 17 months old so it had to be simple and clear.

We would then spend some time meeting her, going to the foster carers' house and watching and learning her routines – feeding, bath, bed and waking up in the morning. This would all take a few days before she would then move in with us. Five days to be exact. It seemed such a short amount of time to get to know each other. Five days! This would all take place in the beginning of the new year, which was only a few weeks away.

We were also told of all the meetings we would have to attend: health visitor and doctor's visits we had to take Billie to and ongoing contact sessions with her birth mother. There was a lot to take in and as I wrote it all down in my notebook I felt a little bit freaked out but mostly surprisingly strong and positive. Of course there were a few niggles of doubt and fear – this was a massive thing and I was only human – but for the moment I refused to let them in. These people needed to know I was completely capable. And I was.

We left the offices and went to the supermarket, picking out things for dinner and the items we had been told to buy for Billie's arrival. Just the fact that our washing powder was going to change to Fairy excited me so much! I loved the fact that we were going to smell the same as the little girl in the photo that we hadn't met yet. I loved the fact that soon she would arrive and stay with us as long as she needed to. On our way home we passed a garden centre lit up with Christmas trees and lights; everything looked shiny and bright, full of that lovely promise of Christmas before it actually arrives. I stopped the car and pulled my husband through the brightly lit doors.

'I know we don't need anything but I just want to get an extra bauble for the tree to signify Billie.'

He smiled and agreed and I found the lightest pink globe. Round and simple and most importantly pink.

Hanging it on the tree that evening I prayed that this time next year I would be doing the same but with a little pair of helping hands, that I'd have a little girl next to me laughing and wishing as she put the fairy on the very top. I prayed that I would be a mother and I prayed that I would have the strength to be a mother for just a little while if that was what was meant to be.

We had a few weeks to get our home ready for our imminent arrival. While most people have nine months to prepare for a birth, we had just a couple of weeks and Christmas was in the middle of all that.

Chris spent the weekend painting the spare room, while my sister and I made trips to Ikea and Mothercare. She was blooming and very visibly pregnant and as we walked into the children's bedroom section of Ikea and picked out rugs, cushions and curtains I could see people smiling at her as if it was all for the baby sitting snug in her tummy, not the one in the photo that was snug in my handbag. I wanted to shout out, 'It's for me actually! It's for my baby!'

My sister had told me six months earlier that she was pregnant. I wrote in my diary at the time: 'Victoria is pregnant at the drop of a hat.' I had already started on our path to adoption and, although I was excited to finally be on my journey, still it had hit me hard. How had she just done it literally a month after coming off the pill? I remember storming blindly out of the house when she told me, yelling at her about the unfairness of life, then driving round the block and ringing her door bell for a second round of screaming before I finally collapsed in a heap and let it go. It was that feeling of being a total failure taking me over yet again. She had been so patient with me, and now I feel so very sorry that what should have been such a happy day for her was overtaken by my selfish emotions.

She had dreaded telling me that she thought she might be pregnant. I had goaded her, saying, 'Well, you need to go and get a test. Shall I go and get you one?' She had tried to say no, desperate not to have to inflict more pain on me by actually doing the test in my presence, but I wouldn't take no for an answer, refusing to hear her. I drove to the chemist, bought the test and sat with her waiting for those two blue lines. The kick in the gut as they shone so clearly. That utter feeling of sadness, of devastation. My beautiful sister had picked me up and cried with me, holding me and stroking my hair, putting her own fears and feelings aside to comfort me. We had got through it together, as we had got through everything in our lives. She felt my pain almost as surely as if it was her own … and now here we were, two 'pregnant' sisters in completely different ways, standing in Ikea!

It's always exciting picking things for newly decorated bedrooms but it's doubled when it's for a child. It's so much fun thinking of what things will look like through their eyes – whether they will like animals or fairies, sheep or sunshine. I didn't want to overwhelm Billie with new stuff so I had borrowed a cot from a friend and my family had given us loads of second-hand toys, but I wanted to get everything just right.

We then drove to Mothercare. This was the moment I had been waiting for, the thing that I had been dreaming of for years. This was my turn to go into a proper baby shop and buy things for my child. I knew that she may not stay mine forever, I knew that she came with a mother and a past but I was going to enjoy this moment and claim it as my own. I grinned at my sister in the seat next to me as we turned into the huge car park. She was so happy for me, so happy to finally be able to share in my joy. I couldn't tell you whose smile was bigger or whose heart was pumping harder. She had waited a long time for this day too!

We walked in, my pregnant sister and I, and I took out my shopping list. Baby blankets, sleepsuits, nappies, baby bath, socks, bedding, plates, cups, bottles, spoons and forks, spouty cups ... the list went on and on. I had loved writing it; I spent hours deliberating over whether to get her patterned or plain sleepsuits. What did I think Billie would like from the little things I knew about her? They told me she was always smiling, a ray of sunshine, and I ended up buying little outfits with smiling suns on them. But the majority of stuff I threw into my trolley was pink! My sister laughed and ribbed me on the fact that I always said I would never be a 'pink mummy' and yet here I was with a trolley full of the colour: pink bibs and pink socks and pink plates. But what if she didn't like pink? I was shopping for a toddler, not a brand-new baby who had no thoughts of its own yet. What if she didn't like any of these things? My sister laughed and assured me that, just like her own two little girls, she would love them. I threw in a few more colours for good measure, just in case, and went to pay for the mountain of baby items I was to take home. I can't express how excited I was to finally own a buggy!

Setting up Billie's bedroom was one of the happiest days I had had for years. The trip to Mothercare and Ikea and then arranging everything in the newly painted room was like catnip to me. We got to bed very late as I couldn't rest until it was all finished. I had bought wall stickers of giraffes and elephants and sunshines. I knew she would have bedding coming with her so I folded her new bedsheets away in her wardrobe for a later date. The colourful rug was set down on the new carpet, a bright-red hippopotamus soft toy lay across it, along with a box of washed and disinfected baby toys that my nieces had grown out of and donated to their potential new cousin. They were seven and ten, old enough to understand that a little girl was coming to stay with us and that we were going to foster her until the courts decided what was best for her. They couldn't wait to meet her and, since we had been very open about adopting and not being able to have babies, I often heard them playing adopters. I would watch them enact the moment of bringing their new children home to look after, though in their heads the situation was more like *Annie* and they would wander through the orphanage picking out their child. A conversation for another day with them!

We took photos for the baby book that was to go to Billie. There was a picture of Chris and me smiling outside our house, a photo of her bedroom, a photo of some toys and books and a teddy called Spencer that we had bought especially for her. It felt bizarre going to the printers and getting them to laminate this odd little book with so few pictures in and just a few words explaining who we were. It was the beginning of me feeling that I constantly had to explain my situation to strangers, even though it was no one else's business. An odd sideways glance or casual question set off the urge in me to explain everything. I really didn't need to but I felt like I had to (more on that later). Suffice to say, the guy in our local printers knew my whole life story and that we were now about to foster a child!

We sent off our book to the foster carers. The bedroom was ready and there was a big basket of toys and baby books in our front room. The next step was to meet the girl herself.

By this point Christmas was well and truly here and we had to wait until New Year's Eve to have our first meeting. We were to drive to the foster carers' and spend a couple of hours there in the morning. The day dawned dark and cold, freezing in fact, and there was snow predicted for the following week. I can't tell you how many tops I tried on before I settled on what was suitable to meet this little girl we were to foster. I didn't want to wear a jumper that was too scratchy or too dark or not colourful enough or too colourful so I looked like a children's TV presenter. I wanted to get it just right.

In the end I put on a pale, soft jumper and jeans. I wrapped the teddy bear we had bought her and tied my hair back so that I looked the same as I did in the photos we sent. Chris and I looked at each other. This was finally happening. Here we were, up and dressed and ready to leave the house and it was ridiculously early. I had hardly eaten a thing I was so nervous. We got in the car and it had started to snow. We had about an hour's drive ahead of us and didn't want to be late so we left loads of time to get there. We arrived in about 40 minutes as it was New Year's Eve and hardly anybody was on the roads. Halfway there I realised I was starving and we ended up sitting in a McDonald's around the corner, drinking tea and wolfing down a Sausage and Egg McMuffin, something I will always remember.

I looked at Chris and asked him if he was really ready to do this. All my fears were whirling round my brain. What if she doesn't like us? What if we can't make her smile or make it OK? What if she hides from us and doesn't speak or just cries? We didn't know what to expect. We had gone through many scenarios in different workshops and were prepared for pretty much anything but at the end of the day you just really want that child to like you. I know we both felt scared and excited but the whole thing also felt hugely weird; we were completely out of our comfort zone. It was almost as if this wasn't really happening to us, that we were playing a part in a film. I think my brain does that in situations that I find pretty surreal – it's like I am almost looking down on myself through a screen. These two people are going to meet a tiny little person and then take her home a few days later. We had no idea how our lives were to change – or indeed whether they were going to change forever or just temporarily.

I remember walking up the steps to the foster carers' house and both of us telling the other to ring the bell. We could hear little squeals of laughter from the other side of the door. Eventually I made Chris ring the bell and we took a deep breath. The foster mother answered the door. She smiled and asked us how we were. Just as we walked into the kitchen a little face appeared behind the baby gate separating the kitchen from the sitting room. She was tiny with little bunches and all dressed up. As soon as we looked at her she disappeared again. And then out of the corner of my eye I would see her reappear, a massive smile on her face, playing peek-a-boo, something we found out was one of her favourite games.

We sat on the floor and Billie came to join us. I had the present of the teddy in my hands and she was excited to open it. She took out her dummy and placed it carefully on the floor beside her while she concentrated on opening her gift. She gave it a big cuddle and said, 'Ahhh,' then put her dummy back in and started to get some other toys out. We read her books and played little games and she showed us her photo album of the time she had been with the foster carers. In every photo she was smiling and happy and she would point to herself and say, 'Billie. Ahhhh.' Neither Chris nor I could take our eyes off this tiny little girl with such a huge amount of energy. She didn't stop! She was constantly up and moving and came and sat on my lap and had a cuddle and a photo for her ongoing memory book. She also showed us the book we had made for her and pointed at us in the photos. The bear that she had unwrapped was smiling at her from one of the pages and I showed her and said, 'Look! Same!' She repeated this, taking out her dummy and using it to point: 'Look! Same!'

I realised then how very difficult it was going to be not to fall in love with her. She smelled of fresh washing and sweet strawberries. I wanted to inhale her! We played with Billie for a few hours, talked to the foster carer about her routine and watched as she changed her nappy and fed her a snack. When it was time for her to have her nap we said goodbye. We would be back to see her in two days' time, to wake her up and give her breakfast. But until then we had to leave her behind. She waved sleepily in her foster mother's arms. 'Bye bye,' she said.

It was funny saying goodbye. I was so excited that we had met her and that she was smiling and cute and really lovely. She had been adorable, properly interacting with us, and my earlier fears had dissipated almost immediately. She hadn't hidden or cried or looked at us with fear. We had all got on really well. I knew I had always got on with children; I enjoyed playing with them and being with them – but I knew that being a mother to them was a whole different thing. At that moment I was just simply relieved that our first meeting had gone so brilliantly, and that this little bundle of energy was so much fun. She was a joy to be around. The enormity of it didn't really hit me until later. I was on my roller coaster at that point. I knew the plan was in place and that it was all about Billie and keeping her settled and trying to keep disruption to a minimum. I had done all the soul searching and it was time now for me to get on with the job in hand and leave 'me' at the door.

For now we had New Year's Eve to celebrate with our friends and family, the beginning of what would be a very exciting and eventful year, whichever way it played out.

The second of January dawned and snow had fallen. The air was quiet and still, with that magical atmosphere that newly settled snow brings. It looked beautiful but meant we had to get up extra early in order to be at the foster carers' in time to wake Billie up. They said she woke between seven and eight usually so to be there at 6.30 a.m. to be safe. We left at 5.30 and drove through the silent, snowy streets, talking and laughing about how depressing it felt to be up so early in the dark. Everyone else was asleep and here we were, driving to wake up a child we hardly knew. Black humour got us through the journey. Would she scream when she saw two over-eager strangers at the foot of her bed? What on earth would she make of it all? I felt for Billie and all the changes that were being brought upon her. We ended up outside the house way too early and made our way to McDonald's again. The McMuffin was definitely turning into a friend!

As we made our way up the steps we laughed at the bizarreness of the situation. The lovely foster carers let us in and we all waited downstairs in the living room with mugs of tea. We had been told what we had to do: smile and say good morning then change her nappy, give her a bottle and bring her downstairs. As we sat and made whispered small talk we heard a little cooing noise from upstairs. Billie was awake!

We took the warm milk ready in the bottle and made our way up to her room. When we opened the door she was standing up in her cot, hair everywhere and dummy in her mouth. We said 'hello, gorgeous' and she grinned and took her dummy out and said 'bot bot', which was her word for bottle.

I took her out of her cot and put her on the changing mat while Chris passed the nappies and wipes and gave Billie her bottle to hold while I changed her. We were actually doing this. Albeit under the eyes of the foster carer but she had very kindly let us do it ourselves, sure that we could manage it. I will be forever grateful to her for the kindness and confidence she showed towards us. We then brought Billie downstairs and fed her breakfast. She was so chatty, speaking in broken words and noises – and very hungry. I couldn't believe how much breakfast she ate. It was lovely to see. After she had eaten we changed her and played for a little while before it was time to leave again. This time we really didn't want to go, it had been so lovely to hear her wake and do all those normal things mothers get to do every single day. I felt as if I would never get tired of it all, the nappy changing and the feeding and playing. It felt real, like it was something I was meant to do. The good news was that we would return later that day to feed her and put her to bed.

We drove home chatting about this funny little girl who seemed so easygoing and welcoming, who actually seemed happy to see us. She hadn't cried or been clingy with the foster carers. She had played with us and sat with us until she got tired and needed her nap. We had a few hours to kill before we had to go back so I called my sister to come over and have a cup of tea.

It was so lovely to talk to her about all the things we had done that morning, discussing mundane tasks that most people take for granted as if they were special treats. I told my sister of my concerns, that in two days Billie was going to come and live with us. What was that going to really be like? Would I be able to do it? She listened and put my mind at rest. She told me I was a natural and to remember what I had always told her, to enjoy all of this bit. This was the end of my weird pregnancy; in a parallel universe I was as big and blooming and about to pop as she was!

That afternoon we made our way back to the foster carers and played with Billie then fed her and bathed her and put her to bed. She was tired and a little more clingy than she had been in the morning but still happy to see us and ate her dinner with gusto! When it was time to bath her we played with her ducks and read her bath books. I loved wrapping her up in a towel, all clean and warm and snug and singing funny little rhymes as I dried between her toes. We put her nappy on and her sleepsuit and settled her into her cot with her bottle. Chris read her a book and we kissed the top of her head as she drowsily closed her eyes while drinking her bottle.

She fell asleep almost immediately and we made our way downstairs for a much-needed cup of tea and debrief. The foster carers thought we were doing well and we drove home exhausted but buzzing with happiness. It was hard to believe that a week ago we hadn't even met her and now this little girl, this firecracker of energy, was firmly making her way into our lives. I couldn't believe how quick the whole process seemed.

The next day we were going to give Billie her lunch and take her out for the afternoon and then stay and put her to bed. We felt as if we had almost moved into the foster carers' home and we were welcomed wholeheartedly. I often thought how strange it must have seemed to them to have these people in their home, showing them a child's routine and helping prepare that child for yet another move. It takes a very special person to be a foster carer; you need a bundle of emotional strength and I knew I was going to have to dig deep myself.

The day after we took Billie out for the afternoon. It was cold and the foster carer suggested a little petting zoo where there was a café. She said we could give her lunch there and bring her back a little later. We had bought a car seat (another truly exciting moment!) and I strapped Billie into it. I thanked God I had a lot of experience of putting my nieces in and out of them and got her in with no trouble. We drove away with her singing in the back. I sat next to her as Chris drove just in case she got scared. I must admit that both of us felt a bit giddy at the chance to be out alone with this little girl. No eyes were on us for the next few hours and we were in sole charge of Billie.

As we got out of the car and strapped her into her brand-new buggy it seemed to get even colder. Snow was still on the ground and Billie was all wrapped up in her snowsuit, hat and gloves but Chris and I were worried she would still be cold so we bought a picnic blanket from the farm shop to put around her just in case. We walked around and looked at the animals and made cow 'moos' and pig snorts, and Billie copied us and laughed. We had lunch in the café. We had packed Billie's favourite things and we sat her in a high chair and fed her mini sausages, cucumber sticks and yogurt. Again that lovely feeling washed over me when I collected the high chair and started feeding her. Little acts that people so often take for granted made my heart properly sing.

After lunch when Billie had had a little run around in the park I could see that she was getting tired – I was already watching her face for the telltale signs. We brought her back to the foster carers' house and sat with her, fed her and bathed her and put her to bed. We were all exhausted and it was lovely to sit on the sofa with her cuddled up on our laps.

On the way home that night Chris and I discussed the fact that in two days we would be collecting her. Tomorrow the foster carers were to bring her to us so that Billie could see her bedroom, play with toys and look around what was to be her new home. We were excited that this strange bit would soon be over. The foster carers were lovely – so kind, helpful and welcoming – but it was also pretty draining getting up and travelling to someone else's house to learn this little girl's routine. Whether you are or not, you always feel like you are on display.

The foster carers and Billie arrived bright and early the next morning. I could hear her outside chatting away and ran down the stairs to open the front door. This was a big moment: Billie was coming to see her new house and I wanted it to be perfect. We had been up late cleaning and sorting stuff the night before and making a last-minute late-night dash to the supermarket for her favourite yoghurts! Billie was really happy to see us and ran into the front room to the basket of toys. Some she recognised from her house as we had been bringing things back with us so that she would feel at home. She started playing with her Fifi and the Flowertots toys and wanting us to play with her.

We then showed Billie her room. She ran into it and hugged Spencer bear that was waiting for her in her cot as she had already seen him in her little book. We showed the foster carers around the house, and they talked me through Billie's favourite food so that I could get everything in for the next day. The foster carers were so kind and confident in everything they did. They told us they would always be on the phone if we needed anything, and to not worry but just go with the flow for the next few days and keep to the routine.

After a couple of hours, we waved Billie off, saying that we would see her the next day and that she would be coming to stay with us. I don't know how much she really understood. She was 17 months old, and she had been moved backwards and forwards a lot of times already in her short little life. She knew a few words but I don't think she had any concept of what was really happening. It was hard for us to take in and we were fully grown adults.

That night, I spoke to Chris about my fears. The next morning we were going to pick Billie up and she would live with us until the courts decided what was best. What was definite was that for the next few months we would have a toddler living with us and that was a massive responsibility.

It wasn't the day-to-day 'parenting' that seemed so daunting but the social workers and meetings and contact. What if we couldn't do it? What if when Billie came to live with us she changed and just cried and we couldn't help her? He said that we could handle it, that we would get used to it quickly as we had with Billie's routine over the last few days. He told me we knew what we were doing and that Billie was lovely. It was going to be OK.

Chris put my mind at rest but I couldn't sleep. I was so excited and scared about what was to come. The fact that Billie would move into our home tomorrow morning was amazing. We had waited for this moment for a very long time. We had chosen in the end one of the hardest routes to parenthood that we could ever choose. We were to be foster carers first. It was temporary but may be permanent. It was and it wasn't. I had to remind myself to just take one day at a time. I was still up in the early hours making lists in the notebook by my bed and writing mantras to myself that I could do this.

We picked Billie up on the Saturday morning. It was still freezing cold but the sun was shining and the sky was bright blue on this beautiful January morning. Billie's social worker was at the foster carers' house to greet us and she told us she would be visiting early the next week. We strapped Billie into her car seat with her dummy in her mouth and her changing bag of nappies and said our goodbyes. I sat in the back seat again with Billie to reassure her but she was waving happily at everyone. As we drove off into the direction of home I smiled. Chris and I looked at each other through the rear-view mirror.

We had done it. We were moving onto the next stage of our lives. Foster carers, not parents yet – but it felt good. It felt like we were free at last! Yes, this feeling would only last for a little while; soon there would be social workers and meetings to attend. But for now, for this moment, it was just us and a little ray of sunshine called Billie.

Perfect roast chicken and roasties

Serves 4

I have said that the smell of roast chicken always takes me back to my own childhood and whenever I cook it – which is a lot – it provides me with an instant warming feeling that tells me that things will be OK. It's a dinner that says 'we are in this together, we are here, we love you'. A true cuddle on a plate.

You will need:

1 whole chicken, weighing about 1.5 kg

1 onion, quartered

1 garlic clove, smashed

Vegetable oil

Salt and pepper

1kg Maris Piper or King Edward potatoes, peeled and roughly quartered

Method:

Preheat the oven to 190°C.

Take a large roasting tin and place your chicken in the middle of it, putting the smashed garlic and half a small glass of water into the cavity of the chicken.

Rub the chook all over with oil and season generously with salt and pepper.

Add the onions to the tin and drizzle with a little oil, then pop in the oven for approximately one hour.

Meanwhile, bring your potatoes to the boil and let them simmer for a two to three minutes. Drain them in a colander and give them a bit of a shake to fluff them at the edges.

Take the chicken out of the oven and baste it with the oil inside the pan, then add the potatoes and toss them in the oil. Season to taste, and cook for a further 20 minutes.

Take the onions and the chicken out of the oven, turning the bird upside down so that the breast is on the bottom, and leave to rest (this keeps all the juices in the breast and stops the chicken from going dry). You can cover them with foil if you like.

Give the potatoes a shake in the tin, turn the temperature up to 200°C, and return them to the oven for a further half an hour until crispy and golden. The chicken will have had a good rest and be ready to serve with the roasties, along with gravy and any veg you like.

Chapter 11

Arriving home with Billie felt like we had won the lottery and found out it was all a joke at the same time.

We felt like a pair of frauds. We had this little girl in our arms, but she wasn't actually ours. At this moment Billie was in the shared care of the local authority and her birth mother; we were simply the foster carers until all the court assessments were completed. As with everyone in this situation, if the child's needs are not being met (for whatever reason), then a placement order would be made and she would be adopted. We had already been approved as foster carers and adopters, so if a placement order was eventually made, and Billie couldn't return home, we could apply to adopt her. But nothing was guaranteed.

We knew the risks involved with concurrent caring. We knew that children placed with concurrent planning carers are not considered likely to be able to return to the care of their birth families. But, until all the court assessments are complete, this is not certain, and a small proportion of these children do return to their birth family or other relatives. There were certain precautions that we needed to take to ensure we didn't all get too attached and because at this point we were officially foster carers. Our names were to be used at all times – we were Lisa and Chris, not 'Mummy' and 'Daddy' and we knew and respected this. While the assessments were being carried out by the courts, as well as giving Billie her everyday care, we would be taking her for regular contact visits with her birth mother and monthly 'looked-after child reviews' with social services, not to mention being on the receiving end of home visits from social workers and district nurses. This certainly wasn't the beginning of us living the parental dream. It was emotional and complicated and delicate for every single person involved and we were all just trying to do our best for this wonderful little girl.

So, in my head this little visitor had come to stay. She needed feeding and warmth and safety, she needed attention and care and stimulation. She needed love and security. She really needed us, and she needed us to step up to the mark and be the grown-ups and not let her down.

That first day we took her to the park and played on the swings, we fed the ducks and then came home and played with her toys. It felt so liberating to be able to make these choices. To be able to just decide to take her to the park, to play on the swings with her. It was a new sense of responsibility, the beginning of a new chapter, whatever the outcome. I felt myself taking deep breaths, to feel that I could actually exhale again.

The weeks before had been so intense, and we were – and would continue to be – under such watchful eyes. But at least a little of the pressure was off and we were being left to find our feet. We gave Billie lunch and dinner and bathed her with her new bath toys and wrapped her in a new pink snuggly towel. We put her in one of her familiar sleepsuits, gave her a bottle in her cot and read her a story. We sang her a lullaby and then waved her goodnight. Both of us smiling and kissing her little head. We followed 'the routine' to the letter. We then turned the lights off, as she liked to sleep completely in the dark, and closed the door.

Chris and I stood on the other side of that door for about 20 minutes, looking at each other and listening to her gurgling into her bottle and singing to herself, hardly daring to move or make a sound for fear that we might disturb her. After about ten minutes, her breathing had become heavy and she sounded like she had drifted off. We waited – no noise – and then a few minutes later we could hear a gentle snoring sound. Billie was asleep. She was actually asleep in our house, in her new cot with her old and new things around her.

We had done it! We had got through the first day. I had made dinner, we had kept her safe, we hadn't done anything to overstimulate her and she had very happily gone to bed, and more importantly to sleep. This was amazing. I loved the fact that my home felt suddenly more alive. It was already like a proper home. We crept away from the bedroom and sat on the top of the stairs. Maybe we would wait a little longer and then open the door and check on her. Another five minutes passed, and we couldn't help ourselves. Billie was indeed still where we'd left her. A beautiful little bundle, fast asleep, looking like she hadn't a care in the world. I looked down at her warm snuggled form. This tiny little stranger. What did she make of us? What did she think of the whole situation?

One minute she was in a foster home, now she was with us, a different set of people looking after her, yet within the space of a day, things felt almost normal. She had seemed to settle so easily and didn't seem at all disturbed by the fact that she was coming to stay with us, though I knew from the work we had done that it would all be in her head somewhere. A whole new world and new people to get used to. I understood looking at her how important the routine must be and how vital it was that she had her familiar sheets and teddies around her. I knew these small things were like a lighthouse to her in a stormy sea, making her feel as safe as she could and guiding her home. I just wanted to cradle her in my arms and tell her it was all going to be OK.

The first few days went like clockwork. We were not allowed to introduce her to friends or family yet, as she had to get used to us and her new surroundings first. Although we were desperate for her to meet everyone, we understood the reasons behind it. We knew there was still a chance she would be returned home to her birth mother, so we tried to manage our expectations and think only about Billie.

Caring for a toddler means you get into a rhythmic routine pretty quickly. Change, eat, play, sleep, repeat. We were so lucky: Billie was super cute and so very easy to look after. She was always chatting, using a language that she had made up, mixed with a few real words and sounds, always pointing to things and asking what they were. It was a sigh of relief to have the whole weekend with no phone calls or social workers. Just us.

Monday came all too quickly and suddenly we had to get ourselves and Billie ready and into the car for a meeting, as well as something called a 'looked-after child review'. That first morning seemed like a military operation, with the alarm sounding and us all having to be ready to leave the house. I suddenly realised the amount of 'stuff' you need with a toddler and I didn't want to be caught out by not having something crucial with me, especially as this would be the first time everybody had seen us together.

I'd checked and double-checked the bags, but hadn't had time to eat any breakfast, so was ratty and nervous in the car. 'Must be more prepared,' I thought to myself.

The social workers (ours and Billie's) met with us to go through what had been happening and to raise any pressing points or questions they needed to ask. This was really just a meeting to see how we were all doing now that the care plan had been carried out and Billie was starting to settle in with us.

Billie ran around and happily entertained the whole room, used to being on display from such an early age. I had to change her nappy in the middle of it and I felt like all eyes were on me as I picked up the changing bag and we headed to the loos. I didn't want to seem too anxious, but I also didn't want them to think I was cocky about it all. After all, she had only been in my care for a few days. I felt like they would be judging everything.

Angela had given me a brand-new changing bag that she had been given (and hadn't used) and I was scared that they would think that I hadn't listened to anything they had said about being very low-key and keeping everything the same. It was just a bag, but I had really wanted to use it; filling it with nappies, wipes, a change of clothes, snacks and a book had brought me so much joy. Yet here I was, almost covering it up so that nobody saw and thought I hadn't kept to the rules. Nobody did see. Nobody batted an eyelid; there was too much paperwork to get through and too many questions to be answered concerning Billie's wellbeing. I would get used to these meetings and they would become almost second nature over the coming months, but for now, it was all so new to me and I was terrified to put a foot wrong. I didn't need to worry, everyone had confidence in me – I had confidence in myself somewhere too, I just needed to find it.

The days that followed were a haze of us all getting used to each other and the new situation. Working out what Billie's different facial expressions or words meant. Noticing when she was tired or needed changing. It was exhausting as I was putting a lot of pressure on myself, desperate to get everything right, to pass the test.

After a few more days, my sister and best friends were finally allowed to meet Billie. We picked the playground so that she wouldn't get too overwhelmed, as there were already loads of children and families there playing and having fun. I wanted the meeting to feel almost accidental, so there would be no pressure or need for stiff introductions. I will never forget watching my sister's face as she and my nieces walked up to us. None of them could take their eyes off the little girl who was running around us, giggling. If I could capture that look of wonder and frame it I would do. My nieces were ten and seven at the time, and they couldn't stop touching her head and helping her on and off the merry-go-round and swinging her on the swings. Watching Billie interact with her potential cousins was properly heart-melting. They were so patient with her and she loved just holding hands and walking with them, staring up at them with wonder. We were told not to spend too much time with new people at first, but it was a truly magical morning. All my dreams seemed to come true at once, but I had to remember that they might only be temporary.

Meeting my dad was another milestone and, as soon as we answered the door to him, Billie picked up one of her books from the shelves and crawled up to sit on his lap and listen to a story. She sat there, happily sucking her dummy and pointing to pictures as he read. This was all I had ever wanted. My dad was so good with her; he had fully embraced being a grandad with my nieces and he was no different with Billie. He wasn't to be called 'Grandpa' so Billie nicknamed him 'Bumpy', trying to copy my nieces who called him Grampy. It stuck!

I felt so grateful that he had done all the family workshops and that he understood the situation – it didn't remotely stop him behaving naturally with her and she felt so at ease. He showed such love and strength and calmness. He told me Billie was a member of our family whatever happened, that if she were to leave, we would always remember her and love her from afar. I loved him for his wise words and his sense of fairness in every situation.

I would find myself laughing and worrying in equal measures at the lengths I went to in order to prove I was worthy of being Billie's 'mother'. Nothing was too much trouble and I tried to pay attention to every detail. My first fixation was writing the food diary of everything Billie ate. The foster carer had done this and I diligently carried it on so that, at every contact and interaction with social services, they could see that she was eating healthily and well. I would worry if I gave her the same lunch two days in a row, in case someone thought that it meant I wasn't bothered. I remember feeling pretty worn out from constantly trying to do everything perfectly. Every item of clothing was washed in Fairy and ironed and put neatly away. Toys were tidied at the end of the day and put away. Nappies were changed and teeth were cleaned. Everything done and documented for the world to see.

It was all going well and those first few weeks flew by, until one morning, I woke to hear Billie's usual singing to signal that she was awake. Instead of smiling at the little voice as I had done every morning before, I felt nothing but fear. I lay in my bed and pulled the duvet around me and just listened. The singing got louder, and Chris woke and asked me if I was going to go and get her.

'I can't' was all I said.

He didn't ask any questions, he just got up and went to her. I could hear them chatting downstairs, him changing her and her asking for her bot bot. I could hear breakfast things being laid out and nappies being disposed of. I heard the television go on and *Peppa Pig* beginning. I just lay there, listening but not moving.

What if I didn't get to keep this little girl, what if I didn't get to hear and see and cuddle this ray of sunlight every morning? What if I couldn't continue doing all that was expected of me? What if we never truly bonded? If she didn't form a proper attachment to me? Still I couldn't move. I felt like I had hit a wall and I just wanted to sleep and not wake up. Chris came and woke me eventually and asked if I was OK. This was so unlike me, I was usually awake and up within seconds of hearing her. I felt embarrassed even saying it aloud, but I told him how scared I was, of the system, of losing her. I told him that I didn't know if I could really do it. He listened. He understood all too well and said he felt the same, but we had a job to do and we had to get on with it.

He wasn't harsh, just pragmatic and calm, and I pulled myself from the bed and into the shower and headed downstairs. I think I went through the motions like this for about a week, but it felt like forever. Chris would get up with Billie while I lay there, paralysed with fear and loathing myself for not getting up, for not being able to be the mummy I had longed to be. I would finally rouse myself and get through the rest of the day, playing with Billie, taking her to the park and feeding her, changing her and cuddling her but not really being present. I felt as if I were living in a daze, every day the same. There I was, really trying to *be* there, to feel things, but I wasn't and couldn't.

The days seemed to drag, and I felt numb and like I was screaming in my head, but the sound was turned to mute. I find it hard even writing this 11 years on. I can't tell you the guilt and the worry I felt. This was what I had signed up for, this was what I wanted, I knew the challenges and possible outcomes ... but I had no idea how it would all really feel when a living, breathing child entered our world. I felt hollow inside, so scared to love her, but knowing deep down that I couldn't stop myself. The minute I saw her little face each day a bit more of my heart was chipped away. Every morning I told myself that maybe if I just stayed in bed for a little while longer I could psych myself up for the rest of the day.

I was so scared of being judged. Even writing this now, I feel that fear again, that someone might be watching and waiting to say that we obviously weren't cut out for the job in hand. Every day I *did* manage to get out of bed, every day I *did* go through all the motions. I managed it, just. But I would fall into bed every evening, exhausted both physically and mentally. I would sleep and sleep, dreading the next day, leaving Billie's waking-up routine to my husband.

Then one morning about a week later, Chris had to go into work for a fitting. We had agreed that I would take a year off work to be the primary carer and Chris had started filming a new show. He left early and I fell back to sleep. I was woken by the little singing voice we had got so used to hearing, but this time there was no one to get her up, just me. I lay there, petrified.

I listened for it again, that little voice, and I knew I had to do this. I pulled on my dressing gown and headed to Billie's room. As I opened the door I found her in her usual position, standing at the end of the cot with her hair sticking up everywhere and her dummy in her mouth. She looked at me and smiled.

'Lisa!' she said, so obviously pleased to see me.

My heart melted.

I wanted to run back upstairs to my bed, to climb back under the duvet and close the door. To not let in this thing that was going to hurt me so very much.

I held my breath.

'Look!' she said, handing me her dummy.

I looked at her little hands offering me her most prized possession. 'Yes,' I breathed. 'Let's get you changed.'

I changed her nappy, gave her a bottle and took her downstairs to breakfast and to watch TV. The usual morning routine. She watched the cartoons but she only really wanted to play with me. I think children are a bit like cats. They have a sort of sixth sense and know if something is up. They know when people are trying to keep a distance, for whatever reason, and almost gravitate towards them. She kept crawling on top of me and asking for my attention. I was singing 'Round and Round the Garden' to her and she kept squealing, 'Again!', 'Again!' I would repeat the rhyme and she would squeal in delight. And then she kissed me on the nose. And we began the rhyme again. And just like that, I was suddenly present. There in my pyjamas, playing with a little girl who looked to me for answers. Who was beginning to look to me for everything.

From that moment my heart had gone. It belonged to her. However difficult the following months would turn out to be, my father's words rang in my ear. She would always in some way be a part of us. I knew that I could do it, that I had to do it. I would be there for her and I would love her, whatever happened next.

During that interaction Chris returned from work. He had quietly witnessed the little scene and taken photos. He captured the moment that I fell in love with Billie. The moment there was no going back. The moment I knew what I had to do. I look at that photo hanging on my wall and tell Billie that was when I fell in love with her. It was only a few weeks into having her, and I knew I had connected with her immediately, but that was the defining moment. The moment I had yearned for and dreaded in equal measures.

As I reread this I feel I want to grab the 'me' back then and hold her tight. I understand of course why I couldn't get out of bed. I see it was self-preservation, I see that it was fear. It was also complete exhaustion. I had been thrown head-first into a brand-new situation and I had hit the ground running. I had put so much pressure on myself to do everything right, to be perfect. Of course I felt the way I did. But I also see that I did do it. I managed to get dressed and keep her fed and looked after and entertained. I managed to do it all while feeling completely overwhelmed by the whole process.

Nothing can really prepare you for it, and under the eyes of social services you put yourself under so much pressure that of course at times you will feel like you are drowning.

It comes in waves, all through your life I think, those moments when you feel you can't quite cope, and with love and support and inner strength you do, until the next wave comes. I think what was doubly hard was that I had wanted this so much. This had been all I had thought about for so long, obsessing over every detail, so I felt like I couldn't turn around to my sister or my friends (or God forbid my social worker!) and say, 'Help, I am struggling.' I felt embarrassed and scared to admit my feelings. I had way too much pride and I couldn't and wouldn't admit defeat. In fact, I told no one of those dark days that seemed to last forever. The only person who knew my true feelings until I was safely out the other end was Chris, and I will be forever grateful to him for pulling me through and holding me up when I couldn't stand.

On reflection, and talking about it later with friends, I was reassured that I was not the only person to go through this. Terror and fear of responsibility are a normal part of new parenthood and it's quite normal for new mothers to feel completely overwhelmed. I was very lucky to have the support network that I did. I got through it and every day it became a little easier.

The winter seemed never-ending, it was a harsh one and we had a lot of snow. One day, coming home from contact, we passed London Zoo. Billie was so excited to see the giraffes' heads poking up from the park that we decided to stop and go in. She was all wrapped up in her snowsuit and hat with big puffy mittens on her hands, but she was so happy to be there. We wheeled her round all snug in her buggy while she looked at all the animals. She couldn't wait to see the giraffes again and watched, mesmerised, as the zookeepers fed them. As we walked through the shop at the end of our visit she spotted a soft toy giraffe. 'Raffe!' she said.

I picked it up and gave it to her and she cuddled it. 'Ah, Raffe,' she said again. From that day on she has slept every night with Raffe. He has been lost and found with the help of Twitter. He has lost most of the stuffing in his neck. He still lives on her bed and is there in times of comfort. I love that she has this cuddly toy and that he is her comfort blanket to this day.

The weeks rolled on. There were home visits from social workers, contact visits to be navigated as well as court dates for placement orders that were constantly being pushed back, as well as mountains of phone calls to make and paperwork to be filled in. In amongst all of this I had to walk the line of 'mothering' my 'daughter' and embracing the toddler groups and Monkey Music, soft play areas and playgrounds. All places where I would meet other mothers, all places where I was never allowed to forget my reality. I hadn't given birth or had a difficult labour, I couldn't join in any of the conversations.

I remember sitting in amongst the balls of a soft play area one morning, surrounded by squealing toddlers, Billie diving head-first and disappearing into a mountain of soft, squidgy balls. After a while, a mother joined me with her little boy.

'She's a one, isn't she?' she laughed.

'Ha, yes she's funny.'

'You've got your hands full there, definitely what I would call spirited!'

I could hear the note in her voice that said it all.

'Has she always been like that?'

I looked over to Billie, who was throwing balls into the boy's face at this point.

'I mean mine was asleep most of my pregnancy, I hardly felt him move but I bet yours didn't stop moving,' she continued.

I smiled and blushed. I remember actually blushing because I couldn't answer her question.

By this point another mum had joined us with two other children and was smiling and nodding at our conversation.

'Oh, don't get me started,' she said. 'I wouldn't go through labour again for anything, it was so awful. I managed to give birth naturally to these two but never again.'

Cue the oohs and ahhs, the talk of doctors and forceps, nothing that I could relate to or even begin to talk about. What struck me was that these children were all over a year old and still it was birth that was being discussed, in gory detail, with absolute strangers.

As I dragged Billie out of the balls and settled her in a high chair to get some lunch, I felt lonely in the sea of mothers and toddlers. I had come to this place to feel a bit more normal and ended up feeling more alienated than ever. I felt as if I were constantly having to explain why she called me by my name, not 'Mummy'. I would tell people that I was fostering her and this would always be met with more questions, a lot of which were so intrusive that I would never have dreamed of asking them of a friend, let alone a complete stranger.

There was also a sense that everybody else could comment on how I was 'parenting' this little girl, as she wasn't really 'mine' in the first place. It was frustrating and I found I had to almost psych myself up and have a stock answer ready when all I wanted to feel was normal. What I've come to realise, looking back, is that these mothers were probably feeling exactly the same way as I was. They had wrapped up their babies and brought them to a play area in order for the children to meet others, and for them to have an adult conversation. Yet the one thing bonding them all was birth, so that was the subject they started talking about. They were all lonely in their own way, trying to figure it out for themselves. Now I can give these mothers a break. Then, I hated them; they seemed more smug than the pregnant women I'd been forced to endure the past few years.

I slowly and surely began to find my feet. My sister had her third baby, Jonny, and I was her birth partner. I had to leave Chris to put Billie to bed and hotfoot it to the birthing unit to witness the most beautiful birth I have ever seen. In all, I have been present at four births and this one was the most magical. My sister had opted for a water birth and a few hours before we had walked up and down the road while we timed contractions, me gabbing away about Billie, trying to keep her distracted. Now here she was with Allen in a big 'pool' with candles lit and music playing. I honestly feel so very privileged to have been a part of that day.

I watched and encouraged as my hero of a sister breathed and pushed with no pain relief whatsoever, until a baby boy 'swam' up to meet us. We were all shocked. We couldn't believe she had made a boy; my sister had been convinced it was another girl and it made the moment all the more special. Allen was crying, my sister was in wonder and she handed him to me – gorgeous, round, perfect and pretty bloody huge! He stared at me with eyes that said *I know you*, and again I melted.

I think it was even more magical to see this baby born as I'd held such a grudge when I had first heard Victoria was pregnant with him. Here he was, ready to take on the world and finally I was in a place where I could cope with it. I felt such a wave of love engulf me. I smiled back at his lovely face. I had a baby to take care of at home and she would need me in a few hours when she woke up.

I became a dab hand at nappy changing, at picking Billie up just as she was about to take a tumble, at caring and loving and cuddling ... but knowing all the while that she might go back to her birth mother. The workshops had stood us in good stead, but it was still quite a harsh reality to face. Every day this little girl did, or learned, something new, every day she was making her way further into my heart and every day I would look at the note that I had written to myself and stuck on the fridge: 'Just for today. What will be will be.'

I also had another note that I carried with me, told to me by my friend Mary. A Zen proverb: 'A snowflake always lands in the right place.' I looked this up for the purposes of the book and the actual proverb is: 'A snowflake never falls in the wrong place.' I love both. Same meaning, different ways of looking at it. It got me through. The harsh reality of concurrent planning meant I was constantly having to remind myself and my family that this child could very well be reunited with her birth mother. I had to remember to make sure no one referred to me as 'Mummy', to make sure that everybody understood. What kept me going, apart from my wonderful family and group of friends, was the thought that I would have helped Billie in some small way.

Believe me, there were days that I struggled to see this, that I berated myself for putting us and our family through this ordeal. I had dreams that the worst-case scenario for me was the best-case scenario for Billie. I pictured how I would cope, envisioned perfectly packed suitcases and boxes of toys. I imagined myself handing Billie back to her mother with my mobile number, asking her to call whenever she needed me, promising endless offers of babysitting and being there if she needed anything at all. That helped to get me through.

Winter turned into spring and then surprised us with snow. We made a snowman in the garden at the beginning of the month and by the end of it we were in sundresses in the garden, filling up buckets with water for Billie to paddle in. She was growing by the day – everyone commented on how she was thriving. The terrible twos arrived early, and we were hit with tantrums and crying. Suddenly the girl who had slept through the night just wouldn't go to sleep and we spent hours outside the door, as we had on her first night, but this time having to go in every few minutes and put her back in her cot, trying to not make eye contact and remain as calm and quiet as possible. Easier said than done but I honestly loved nearly every minute of it. I felt like I was actually a parent. I could finally join in the conversations about my child not sleeping or the trials of potty training, conversations I had been desperate to be a part of, which I now didn't have to sit on the edges of.

I think one of the hardest and most frustrating things for everyone involved was the fact that the court dates were constantly being adjourned. The local authority thought that it was in Billie's best interests to be adopted and for us to continue caring for her. But assessments were still being carried out and it was the court's final decision. I understood that the courts needed all the evidence possible as this was a child's life we were talking about, but it was hard for everyone involved not knowing what was going to happen for so long. We were all walking a constant tightrope of uncertainty. I'd call my sister when Billie was napping, asking her to counsel me through it all. To tell me the words that I needed to hear and to give me the strength to keep on keeping on.

Court dates were finally put in place and we waited to hear our fate. As with every part of this process, it's a double-edged sword, with a child at the centre of it who everyone wants to love.

Billie was one of the lucky ones; everybody in her life adored her and wanted to look after her and they continue to do so.

It is the same for everyone going through concurrent planning – throughout the whole process everybody involved on all sides is continuously and independently and rigorously assessed. Ultimately, the paperwork and evidence is presented to a family court judge for consideration and ruling. Eventually the courts decided that it was in Billie's best interests to be adopted, and I have to say that this really was a bittersweet moment and one that took me by surprise.

I recognised that this was desperately sad that Billie wouldn't live with her birth mother, that she wouldn't be able to be cared for by her. But that ruling meant that the plan for Billie was adoption, with or without us and, however sad it was, we were committed and excited to apply to adopt her and officially become her parents. We also felt genuine happiness that Billie wouldn't have any more moves or new people to get used to. She would be with us for good.

This had been the longest and hardest thing we had ever done. IVF and an ectopic pregnancy seemed like a walk in the park compared to the ups and downs of the past eight months. Our emotions had been tested to the limit, and – finally – we were going to get the chance to be fully legitimate parents. After years of stress and torment, of despair and wanting, my prayers had been answered and I was going to be a mummy. The joy I felt in those few words was uncontainable. We were to become a forever family.

Rice Krispie Chicken

In the days before chicken nuggets, my mum used to make these for my sister and me. One of the best things about having a toddler was that I could finally do all the things that I had dreamed of doing with her, cooking being one of them. This is one of the first things I cooked for Billie. She loved baking and also helping make these when she was little, and they are still one of our go-to comfort foods when she or I feel the need to be wrapped up and looked after a little more than usual. I had to put these in this book as making them stirs up memories from so many times in my life – making them with my own mother and then recreating them with my daughter.

Serves 4

You will need:
250g Rice Krispies
Mayonnaise for dipping
4 skinless and boneless chicken breasts, cut into nuggets or goujons
Salt and pepper

Method:
Preheat oven to 200°C/gas mark 6.

Put the Rice Krispies and salt and pepper into a large bowl and crush with your fingers.

Put a big dollop of mayonnaise on a plate.

Dip the chicken first into the mayo and then into the Rice Krispies. Then place onto a baking tray lined with grease-proof paper.

Bake in the oven for about 25 minutes until golden and serve with potato wedges and ketchup.

Chapter 12

This really is the beginning of the narrative. Many people would think that this was the happy ending, the end of the story, and to some extent it is, but it is also the very beginning. The start of life together as a family and the beginning of the healing process for our daughter.

I will start with the end of the beginning of the story.

After further court dates for adoption orders and us going to a matching panel for Billie, now we had to be officially matched with Billie. With that part all done and dusted, it was really a case of filling in more forms and meeting with a panel of experts. This was much the same as the original adoption panel. We would be asked to talk about our time with Billie and why we thought we would make good parents for her.

We were still jumping through hoops and, though it remained utterly exhausting, this time there was a very definite light at the end of the tunnel. It was much easier knowing that we were nearly there. It was the first time I went to a panel feeling properly confident. I had been caring for Billie for ten months and felt I could answer any question thrown at me about her. I knew her routine, though it had changed somewhat over the past few months. I could talk about new challenges we were facing such as potty training and finding nurseries, but above all, I could speak about her with true love.

We were called a little later that day to say that we had been matched, that now we could officially apply to adopt her. Again, paperwork to be filled in and time to be taken, but eventually all of it was done. Billie was officially adopted and we had a final court hearing with a family judge to make it all official. What a joy that day was. It was just for our family to attend so my sister and her family, my dad, my grandma and all our in-laws came to celebrate with us. The judge gave Billie a special soft cuddly toy dog that she immediately called Judge. We had photos taken and, as I looked around at this wonderful family of ours, I felt truly blessed. Our little girl was forever part of this wonderful family, this supportive team that would never let her fall. Everybody was so very happy, excited to be bona fide grandmas and grandads, aunties, uncles and cousins and, of course, we were finally Mummy and Daddy. To earn that name was truly a special moment. I was sad that my own mother wasn't there to share in this momentous day, but I knew she was there in spirit. Grandma Julie would have loved Billie.

We celebrated with lunch and a trip on the London Eye. Billie was too young to fully understand what was happening, but she was aware of how very special this day was and that she was the star attraction, with everyone toasting her and cuddling her. We always celebrate her adoption day; I think it means more to her the older she gets and the more that she understands her story.

I had finally become a mother and life continued. It hadn't come easily, it hadn't come in the textbook way I had dreamed about, but here I was, a mother of a two-year-old and my day-to-day life was much the same as my friends, all of whom had toddlers around the same age.

I think one of the hardest things about infertility is that there's a timescale. Your friends are all around the same age when that biological clock starts ticking, so wherever you look, all your peers are doing what you are so desperate to do. I don't have the answers on making peace with this. I only know that my peace came when I became a mother. It's a tough one and I will never judge how people come to terms with this or don't. A friend gave me the best piece of advice, which was to stop looking at everyone else's ladder while I was climbing my own, as it would only make me wobble and fall off. Wise words. All I know is that we all find our way eventually.

Maybe it's about belonging. I wanted to belong, and I felt very happy to belatedly belong to that club. It didn't matter how I had got there, and, although parenting a toddler had its hurdles, I would never take it for granted.

Our daily routine was one I had dreamed about for years. I would wake and watch *Milkshake!*, we would get dressed and I would take Billie to a music group or to the park. We would have lunch and she would have a nap. We were constantly busy and I loved it.

Of course there were days when she would have massive tantrums and frustrating nights when she wouldn't sleep, despite all the rocking and driving around. I remember one night we stayed over at my dad's house and Billie slept in the spare bed with me. Every time I opened my eyes to check on her she was awake, these wide eyes staring back at me like huge dark saucers. There was no sleeping happening and, after another hour of stroking her hair and singing lullabies, I lay staring at the ceiling, completely frustrated with myself and Billie. What was wrong? Why wouldn't she sleep? I had tried everything. As I lay there going through a mental checklist it dawned on me that the reason she might not sleep in this new bed was because she wasn't sure where she was or what exactly was happening. I went from being angry and frustrated to understanding and seeing it all so very clearly through her eyes. I packed up our bags, wrote my dad a note and drove home. She needed to sleep in her own bed, she needed to know where she was. I needed to be more patient and explain things more clearly, not an easy task with a toddler.

It was the same a few months later when we went on holiday; we had to explain the situation and act it out with dolls. In fact, my one greatest piece of advice is to get a dolls' house. It's brilliant for playing out normal situations and helping children understand. It certainly helped us deal with her worry about going on holiday and allowed us to explain that we weren't moving there permanently and that we would always be coming home.

I have to say that I relished it all. I loved the fact that I could walk into Mothercare or Gap at the drop of a hat and buy clothes for my girl. I had no qualms that she loved dressing up and most days she was dressed as a Disney princess or Buzz Lightyear. I learned not to sweat the small stuff. Who cared if she wouldn't wear 'normal' clothes and had to wear wellies with every outfit?

We painted and glued and played music and danced and sang. We fed the ducks and went to swimming groups, we lay on the sofa and read *Goodnight Moon*. Those days were so precious, and I loved just hanging out with her. But all too quickly she needed to go to nursery and I had to share her again.

It's funny because even as Billie started nursery I still felt the need to explain myself, especially to other mums who still seemed to want to talk about births! When was this ever going to stop? Eventually I became adept at answering only people that I liked, realising that the whole world didn't need to know everything. Although you feel that you're somehow being dishonest if you don't explain your situation in full. It's understandable, after all the explaining you have had to do to get to the place you are, but it's nobody else's business. It's not that you are being rude; it's a bit of self-protection. I was always (and probably still am) so worried about what people would think, but you have to let that go.

As with most children, there were challenges ahead, especially when it came to researching which nurseries would best suit Billie's needs. She was super active, and a quiet nursery would not have worked for her at all. Her attachment to me had grown very strong and for a while she hated to be left. I was constantly and patiently reassuring her that I would be coming to collect her, that I would be coming back. The long-ago phone call to the adoptive mother kept coming back to me. 'Parenting plus' was a good way to express it. There was all the everyday parenting and then there was the 'plus'. There were the effects of trauma on Billie that would need to be explained to teachers. There were doctor's appointments and certain questions that I couldn't answer, as I didn't have the information.

And then there was the ongoing life story work. Trying to help Billie make sense of her story, age appropriately. Using dolls and drawings to tell her of her birth family and where she came from. An ongoing conversation that will never stop and one that we are committed to honouring.

At the end of the adoption process you almost want to hide from the social workers and workshops on offer. Believe me, after so long you have had your fill. You want to be able to get on with the business of being your family, of creating your bond and being confident in your parenting. Only time can do that and, for a while, you will hunker down and not ask for help unless it's really needed. It takes a while, and when I say a while I mean at least a year, to feel that you are not being watched or judged. That you are a parent, that you know what is right for your child.

In the blink of an eye, Billie had started school, and it was one of the proudest and most emotional days of my life.

There she stood for her obligatory photo outside the front door, dressed so very smartly in her brand-new uniform with a big smile on her face. As I waved her off, I cried and cried outside the school gates and on the walk home. The beginning of a new chapter, of new friends and of not being the only person to influence my growing girl. She had skipped in and was so happy and excited and here I was, a heap. I should have been congratulating myself a little on the fact that she felt ready to go to school to start this new adventure. Instead I couldn't stop crying at the thought that life was flying by far too quickly. I wanted to put the brakes on a bit. I felt like I had only just got her and was now losing her to the rest of the world. She loved school and her teachers, she did well in her reception class and, thankfully, for the first time ever, school-gate chat with other mothers was based on the here and now and not their births.

I breathed a huge sigh of relief at the little things. Navigating school and friends with an adopted child has been interesting. Billie's schoolfriends' views of adopted children were of babies in cots in old-fashioned orphanages or, as I've said before, the things they've learned from *Annie* or Jacqueline Wilson books. There are always those difficult moments – like the family trees that schools still insist on doing, which always cause a stir. But in the main, schools have been very supportive, offering help wherever they can. If you're in this situation yourself, there is a lot of help on offer out there with a government grant called Pupil Premium. Don't be afraid to ask for it.

I have been very blessed along the way to build up a support network of other adoptive parents. It is worth noting that, although your child will have the same issues as her peers and your own friends' kids, adopted children will always be a little different and need parenting differently. At the beginning, people may try to discipline your child for you (usually because they feel that they somehow have the monopoly on mothering as they physically gave birth), and it probably comes from a well-meaning place, but that's when you really have to be strong.

Adopted children come with their own special set of circumstances and putting them on the naughty step may cause all sorts of issues. Talking to other adoptive parents is always a sigh of relief. Whenever I meet anyone who has adopted there is a sort of unspoken language between us. We just get it. There is no judgement and it is so refreshing to feel that you are not alone. There is always that 'plus' ringing in your ears. I also know that this can be a hard road to travel and you need as much support as you can get. I have not been afraid to ask for help at times.

I think one of the real differences and difficulties of raising an adopted child is that you are constantly questioning what's developmental and what's a result of being adopted. Again, well-meaning friends will tell you that your child is exactly the same as their child or someone they know, but that's not always the case. There is now huge research on the effects of trauma on an adopted child and it can present itself as being very similar to ADHD, FASD and what some people may call just 'naughty' behaviour.

There are lots of great books and talks about this and, as you stick your head over the parapet and start to own your motherhood, you will see that there is a wealth of workshops and support groups that I promise will be invaluable as your children grow. Please know that this is not as awful as it sounds. The day-to-day parenting continues, the play dates and homework and friends, but every now and then I am notified of a workshop or a support group and something resonates with me and I go. I usually feel a million times better afterwards, and feel that I am always doing 'homework' to help my daughter.

The 'plus' continues in the form of birthdays, Christmas and Mother's Day. All of these occasions have been bittersweet, as all these dates hold a more complex meaning for an adopted child. Even if they have no clear memories of being with their birth family, they know that they were born to someone else and this will bring a mix of emotions on days like Mother's Day. This all happens as they grow a little and understand their story more clearly. It's worth knowing that these days will always be somewhat difficult and sometimes not the picture -perfect events you had planned in your head, but then what is? I've learned to go with it, to not build these events up too much. To understand there are two sides to every story.

So what else have I learned about adoption, that could help anyone thinking about it?

I have learned that you are not born a mother. You become a mother; you have to earn it. It is not as simple as just giving birth. It is the hours of the mundane and the hours of caring. The times spent really listening to what your child has to say, the knowledge that you will not always be able to fix everything but you will always be able to help heal.

I have learned that life story work, like parenting, is ongoing and revisited frequently. That is not to say your own family life is undermined or ruled by this, but it has to be taken into consideration. Sometimes children want to deal with their past and sometimes they don't. They can ask the most awkward questions at times you least expect (usually while you're driving somewhere) and you just have to take the opportunity and try to answer as best you can. Mostly they just want to live in the now, to be considered normal and not have to worry about it all. There's a real balance to be had between talking about it too much and not enough. Life story work changes as children grow up and understand more about their early life. It is not to be shied away from. The more open and understanding you can be, and the more you can hold their hand and offer support throughout their questions, the better it is for them. Knowing that your role will always be to be their mum, whatever lies ahead in the future, and that you will hold their hand alongside their birth family, is a great source of comfort to them.

I feel like maybe I love my daughter even more than if I'd made her myself. I do sometimes overcompensate and I know I'm constantly wanting to make everything better. I would like to be able to take control of every sticky situation she finds herself in so that she doesn't have to, but I know that it's not possible and that I just have to be there if and when she falls.

I made a promise to her and I will not let her down. I think I love with more ferocity than I ever thought possible.

A truly wonderful thing about the fact that I didn't make my daughter is that I can fully celebrate her. She is beautiful and I am in wonder of her. I don't see my own features smiling back at me, but I see my mannerisms at the times I least expect. I can always reply wholeheartedly without seeming conceited, 'Yes, she is beautiful, isn't she?!'

I suppose because we don't have blood bonding us, I am always fascinated by family resemblance. I see that must be hard for my daughter at times, where everyone comments how we look alike or how alike her cousins are to their mother. I can't take my eyes off mothers' or fathers' and siblings' children that look so alike. I look at my new husband-to-be and all his children and see how it's in their gait, their smile, the way they read a book or wake up in the morning, and I am fascinated.

I have learned that I am the adult. It's a huge lesson and sounds as if I'm stating the obvious, but a lot of people don't think or act this way when it comes to their kids. Whatever age they are, they are still the child and you are the adult. It has stood me in good stead. It means that I will always be the person to come to even when I feel like I want to be the child and scream and shout!

And yet, it could be argued that maybe the 'plus' is just parenting. I look around and every parent seems to have a cross to bear, their 'bit' to deal with. Maybe my conclusion is that it's all relative and there is no real difference between parenting a birth or adopted child, except that there is just a bigger cast of characters you have to deal with.

It also is clear as I struggle with this last chapter that, of course, I will struggle because it is not the end. The story continues, and the healing is ongoing, because it is never really over. Every step of my journey produced a new hurdle that I thought was the hardest, only for it to be usurped by the next challenge. Getting pregnant, having an ectopic, failing IVF, not getting pregnant, becoming an adopter, becoming a mother, the toddler years, the primary school years, and now adolescence. With all of these challenges comes a deep breath and a look to the sky to say: 'How am I going to deal with this one?'

I have to let go of all of the shame that I felt for so very long. Shame at not being able to do the one thing that so many women take for granted. Shame at not being able to have a baby. Shame at feeling that I wasn't good enough. I had to let it all go. If I'm really honest, I don't think I will ever be completely free of that pregnancy pipe dream. Even though I know that I don't work in that sense, and that I am almost too old to have a child let alone want another one, I think that slight hope will be with me every month until my periods stop and I physically can't have a baby, because nature has stepped in and stopped it for good.

I have to trust in everything that got me to where I am now. Trust in what's guiding me forward. It's all such a complicated story with many, many players and the only thing that has got me through it is love, from my amazing network, my tribe of family and friends, books and quotes and the never-ending journey of my love for a child who became my daughter.

There are no guarantees as to how anyone's story is going to play out, how a child's life is going to be, whether birth, assisted, surrogate, fostered or adopted. There is always a new patchwork in my daughter's tapestry, in all of our tapestries, to help mend and the only way I know how to do that is with love.

So, I give true thanks, to all the circumstances that have occurred in my life and all of the people involved in my life, that have allowed me to be where I am right now. From the bottom of my heart.

'A snowflake never falls in the wrong place.'

Zen proverb

Epilogue

Eleven years on and so much has changed.

I am mother to a 12-year-old. She is practically a teenager and with that comes the trials and tribulations of normal adolescent behaviour. Big changes to navigate, like secondary school and new friends, goalposts moving and more freedom. My daughter understands her story more and more. We are very open about everything and we talk about adoption a lot.

Life has changed: divorce, new families, step-families. Great-grandparents have passed on and new family members have been born. One thing that hasn't changed, and will never change, is my love for my girl. Since the time of that first photo that sits proudly in a frame in my bedroom until now, our love has grown stronger and stronger. I am her mother, her mama.

My snowflake landed and found me and, though there have been (and will be many more) ups and downs, we are forever bound together, an invisible line between our hearts. Nothing will break that wonderful bond I share with my daughter. I will share her with many, including her birth mother, and I'm happy with that. She is so truly amazing, how could I keep her for myself? I want her to shine, for everyone to see the brilliant spark that she is. She is part of me, of my nurture and very much part of her nature. She is her own person and a person to be celebrated. I love every single piece of her and everybody that made her, I accept all that she is and all that she comes with. I hope that all the good things I've taught her will rub off and stay with her, as all the things my mother taught me have stayed with me. Now she's practically a teenager, I am always texting her quotes like 'You can do it' and 'Be kind'.

I hope that her childhood will be full of mostly happy memories, the things that make us: family dinners, birthdays and holidays in the sun. Walks in the woods with the dog, baths, hot chocolate and lullabies. Curling up on the sofa watching TV together. Falling over and catching her as much as possible, crying and laughing and singing in the car at the top of our voices. Parents' evenings, exams, washing uniforms and tidying bedrooms. Cuddles and kisses and saying: 'I love you more than I knew was possible.' As her mother I am a taxi service and a shoulder to cry on, someone to scream at and be angry at when that hole in her soul hurts and hurts. Someone to listen to her and to really hear what she is saying. The person to guide her and help her and to be the boundary she desperately needs to kick against. Her safe place. A champion of all the things she does, a champion of all the things she is.

I will always be there to walk alongside her and to help her fill in the gaps when she is ready. I will help her and hold her hand throughout her teenage years and on and on into adulthood, until I no longer exist except in the blue skies of the summer and the grey of a rainy day.

I never thought I'd say this, but now I wouldn't change my infertility for the world, as without it I wouldn't have met my girl. My wonderful, brilliant, beautiful, funny, clever, full-of-life Billie.

In 2017 there were 72,670 children in care, and
4,350 children were adopted from care.

Acknowledgements

Thank you to Ebury and my fantastic editor Robyn Drury for believing in my very personal book and having the same vision as I had. You have been so very supportive and always there for me.

To Carly Cook, a massive thank you from the bottom of my heart. I don't think I could have written this book without you. You care as much as I do, thank you for holding it so carefully and for really listening. Thank you for the questions and the lunches, I thoroughly enjoyed every minute, even the crying! You are a true friend.

To Jonny McWilliams my agent and my friend, thank you for taking my call from the pub late that Friday afternoon and for really listening to what I had to say and for always believing. We make a great team.

A big, heartfelt thanks to Chris Terry.

To everyone I have written about in the book I am very grateful.

To Chris, thank you.

To my unwavering lifeboat of a Sister and my superhero of a Daddy. I would be nowhere without you.

My bestest friends Emma, Ange (you made this happen!) and Nicola.

My Auntie and my Godmothers, Mr Taranissi, and to Coram.

To Mary, thank you for letting me tell the world about your brilliance.

To Lou and Net for reading and for your thoughts, advice and for all our conversations and for your sunshine.

To Nadia, that phone call that morning. You inspire me.

To my John for your constant belief in me. You teach me to keep striving to be the best I can be. I love you.

To my Mother Julie and my Daughter Billie for completing the circle.

And most of all I give my heartfelt thanks to every single situation that brought me to where I had to be, for what was meant to be.